The World is a Wedding

A. M. ALLCHIN

THE WORLD IS A WEDDING

Explorations in Christian spirituality

New York
Oxford University Press
1978

First published in Great Britain in 1978 by
Darton, Longman and Todd Ltd.

First published in the United States in 1978 by
Oxford University Press
New York

From *Collected Poems* by Edwin Muir.
Copyright © 1960 by Willa Muir.
Reprinted by permission of Oxford University Press, Inc.

From "Little Gidding" in FOUR QUARTETS, copyright, 1943,
by T.S. Eliot, renewed, 1971, by Esme Valerie Eliot.
Reprinted by permission of Harcourt Brace Janovich, Inc.

Library of Congress Cataloging in Publication Data

Allchin, A   M
The world is a wedding.
Includes index.
1. Spirituality.   I.   Title.
BV4501.2.A38   248   78-16888
ISBN   0-19-520079-9

Printed in the United States of America

'Nothing that exists is an island unto itself; . . . everything that holds membership in the world is an element of a seamless garment – the 'ragged edges' of every individual reality splay off into those of another, and the world is a wedding.'

Nathan Scott

Acknowledgements

Of the essays collected in this book, the Introduction and chapters 1 and 2 have not previously been published. Chapters 3 and 8 were first published in *Sobornost*, chapters 5 and 6 in *Christian*, chapter 9 in *Cistercian Studies* and chapter 10 in *Theology*. Chapter 7 forms part of *Solitude and Communion* published by SLG Press. Chapters 1 and 2 were originally delivered in 1976 at General Theological Seminary, New York, in a special Bicentennial Series of lectures entitled 'Spirituality and the New Consciousness'.

The author is grateful to the following for permission to quote copyright material: Christopher Davies Ltd for 'Tyred Allan' by Bobi Jones; Faber and Faber Ltd for 'The Sleeping Lord' by David Jones; J.D. Lewis and Sons for 'Flesh and Spirit' by Gwenallt; to the SLG Press for permission to print chapter 4.

Patri Reverendo
Amico Dilectissimo

DUMITRU STANILOAE

Divinae Veritatis
Antistiti Maxime Perito

Contents

Introduction

The essays in this book are primarily concerned with what is called spirituality. They seek, however inadequately, to do justice to the unfathomable mystery of human life, particularly when it is lived in a growing realisation of the presence and power of God. It is furthermore Christian spirituality which is here under discussion, the Christian faith as actually lived and prayed, the life of God in the life of man, the life of man's spirit transformed and renewed in the coming of the Spirit of God. This does not altogether exclude a consideration of the other great religious traditions of mankind. Indeed, as is suggested in the first essay, it seems probable that the Christian tradition will not be able to develop and grow in the future except as it begins to enter into a living interaction and exchange with those other traditions. But that is the subject for another book.

What is written here has been prepared for varying audiences in varying situations over the course of the last fifteen years. Behind all the essays there are certain settled convictions which while they have grown during this period have not undergone any fundamental change. The first relates to that sense of the mystery of things of which we have already spoken. It insists that only an attitude of humility and respect is appropriate before the deep things of man, and only an attitude of humility and worship before the deep things of God. This is where we must begin if we would come to know God, in silence and amazement. To say this does not mean that there is no place for the use of man's critical and analytical faculties in these matters. It does mean that those faculties can never have a

first place in them. For if there is a God it is certain beyond all
things that man cannot be in a position to judge or dissect him. Not
thus could we begin to know him.

That there is a real knowledge of God open to man, all that is
written here would wish to assert. But it is a knowledge which demands the whole of our assent, not that of the reasoning intellect
alone. It is a knowledge which is always tempered with awe,
'instinct' as Dean Church remarks of the theology of Lancelot Andrewes 'with the awful consciousness of our immense and hopeless
ignorance of the ways and counsels of God.' [1] It is a knowing in
unknowing. When Samuel Palmer first visited William Blake, the
old man asked him how he approached the work of painting. 'With
fear and trembling' came the reply. 'Then you'll do' responded the
master. How much more should this be true of theology, the art of
arts, the science of sciences.

There follows from this an unfashionable respect for the given
elements of Scripture and tradition. Not that they are to be treated
with blind or slavish reverence, but that they are to be accepted as
forming part of a coherent whole, the full scope and range of which
is not altogether open to our investigation. There is a resolute refusal
to reduce or accommodate the roughness of the data to the requirements of our late twentieth-century mentality, and an uneasy sense
that there may be important things to which our age is blind. If we
are to come to know God it will be we who have to change, to
adapt ourselves to his requirements. 'Who are we,' as Mr Keble exclaimed in a slightly different context, 'that *our* satisfaction, *our* com-
fort and ease of mind should be the regulating point (if one may so
call it) of the machinery of God's dispensations? The index whereby
to determine in what measure and degree the Almighty shall have
revealed himself to his creatures?' [2] It is only as we are beginning to
enter in that we shall begin to understand. The Christian tradition is
not something to be understood from outside. The knowledge of
God can grow in us only in so far as we are seeking to conform our
lives to the revelation of God's will for us; in Christian terms only
in so far as we are willing to enter into and participate in that community of love and knowledge, of faith and experience which is
called the Church. Here again the attitude which is asked of us is
not one of blind and slavish submission; it is one of respect and

diffidence before the accumulated experience of the centuries, a willingness to let our eyes be opened to new and disturbing realities.

And here a further conviction intervenes, a sense that we live in an age which while it is rich beyond belief in certain areas of human achievement – who would have thought that we should walk on the surface of the moon? – is strangely impoverished in other and perhaps more vital matters. Only to read the writings of a Richard Hooker or a Maximus the Confessor, a Symeon the New Theologian or a Julian of Norwich, to take a few names from widely different parts of the tradition, is to feel oneself in contact with men and women who were part of a society which, whatever its own limitations and poverties may have been, had a sense of the things of God which is not easily realised in our own age. This sense of our littleness before the tradition has been enhanced for the writer by the experience of living under the shadow of Canterbury Cathedral. The magnificence of such a building speaks of an age which had an insight into mysteries and meanings which we now scarcely glimpse. It curiously relativises the pretensions of the twentieth century. We certainly do not want to indulge in a romantic nostalgia for the past. Our own age is potentially as rich as any other in possibilities of coming to know God. It has its own particular gifts and glories which we should seize upon and appreciate. But we also do not want to be caught in that temporal parochialism which afflicts many of our contemporaries, the approach which in Christian terms 'despises and ignores the human experience of the believing community from whenever it emerged into history after Abraham, until, say, the time of Schleiermacher.' [3]

The spirituality which is described here is therefore rooted in a tradition of faith and experience of many generations. It is a living stream of what David Jenkins calls in the book just quoted, 'corporate knowing'. It assumes, against a good deal of current writing, that through all the diversity of the writings which go to make up the Old and New Testaments there is an underlying unity which reflects on the one side 'the human experience of the believing community', and on the other the activities of God who makes himself 'known to be act, gift, love'. These two elements of the initiative of God and the response of man find their central nodal point in the person of Jesus himself in whom God and man come out from them-

selves to meet in a new and unlooked for unity of love, so that in
some sense we may say that the writings of the two Testaments find
their coherence and unity in him. What is true of the diversity of experience in the two thousand years covered by the biblical narratives
is no less true of the two thousand years covered by the history of
the Church. In and through the diversities, indeed in and through
the tragic separations which have marred its life in so many ways
'the human experience of the believing community' has continued.
Here too there is an underlying unity of faith and prayer, of love
and knowledge. All Christians have let their prayer be shaped by the
Lord's Prayer, have sought to follow the Lord's injunctions in their
attitude towards their neighbour. Nearly all have followed the command he gave to his disciples on the night before he suffered to do
this in remembrance of him. The great majority have confessed their
faith in the terms of the apostles and the fathers, believing that
Christ is truly God and truly man, and that the Spirit whom they
have received is no less God than he is.

   In joining together the apostles and fathers in this way we are, of
course, flying in the face of a large part of the received opinion of
the scholars during the last hundred and fifty years. It has been
thought possible, necessary even, to drive a wedge between the
writings of the apostles and those of their successors, and within the
New Testament itself between the apostolic writers and their
master. The results of doing this, from the point of view represented
in this book, have been disastrous and destructive. The whole makes
sense; the parts in separation do not. The formulations of the early
centuries, culminating in the definition of Chalcedon by which so
many Christians have lived over since, far from being a betrayal of
the substance of the Gospel are a faithful and inspired transposition
of its contents from one cultural milieu to another. They do not
preclude the possibility of further transpositions in the future; rather
they encourage them, providing as they do a paradigm and model of
such creative moves of interpretation. That such new transpositions
are urgently needed in our own day may almost go without saying.
The sadness of our present situation is that much of the more
original and daring thinking on this subject takes place on the mis-
taken premise that we have to go back behind Chalcedon, behind St
Paul and St John to some supposed original message, which when

we reach it always turns out to be immeasurably poorer than that plenitude of faith in Jesus as Lord and Saviour, which the Christian centuries have professed.

There is at this point a further conviction about the nature of development as it occurs in the life of an individual or a nation no less than of a whole tradition. As Thomas McFarland remarks in his massive study of Coleridge 'We too often think of "development" as a kind of progress up a series of steps, the improvement of one's position by the abandonment of a previous position. Actually the word implies an unwrapping of something already there. Its sister words in German and French suggest the same psychological truth. *Entwicklung* implies an unwrapping, *épanouissement* a flowering from a bud.' [4] This is surely pre-eminently true in the case of the Christian tradition. All is given in principle from the very beginning, whether we think of the ninety years which stretch from the birth of Jesus to the writing of the fourth Gospel, or even of the first moments of death, resurrection and the coming of the Spirit. It may well be that there are stages in the process of unwrapping, in the flowering of that original gift which as yet we can scarcely even conceive. We are only at the beginning of the Church's history. But the possibility of growth into the future is bound up with the faithful recollection of what has already been given in the past. The original events of the Gospels constantly reassert their power and creativity in a variety of unexpected ways. We are always, if we are true to their message, becoming contemporary with them.

In this book, we are not for the most part concerned with the areas of the tradition crystallised in the Old Testament nor indeed directly with the centre of the picture as given in the New. But this does not mean that the New Testament witness is absent. Rather it is seen in and through the witness of the saints. One of the underlying presuppositions of these pages is that the lives of the saints provide a most important resource for understanding and interpreting the gospel narratives. It is a constant source of surprise that so little attention is paid to these records by those who attempt to elucidate the writings of the evangelists. The problems of the miraculous in the first century, for instance, could be illuminated from the problems of the miraculous as they confront us in the nineteenth century in the lives of a St Seraphim or a St John Vianney, when the documentary evidence is so much more ample. For clearly the first disciples were men caught up in a moment of supreme religious activity and illumination. It is through men who have been involved in similar if lesser moments of experience that we are most likely to learn how they thought and felt and acted, and are most likely to be freed from the limitations of vision which our age imposes on us, without our being aware of them.

The importance of a close scientific study of the original texts is not being questioned here. Its value has been amply proved in the last one hundred and fifty years. But that way of approach has its own limitations and needs to be supplemented by others. To hear the scriptures read in a community of prayer and praise is to receive another and no less valid impression of their meaning than that which we receive through their academic study. It is to learn to hear the words with our bodies as well as our minds. The detailed study of the text of Shakespeare is no substitute for the insight to be gained through the actual performance of the plays. It is in their liturgical use that the Scriptures come to life.

Thus in this book we assert not only the unity of Scripture and Tradition within themselves but also their unity with each other, through all the human diversities which historical studies rightly bring to our attention. And this unity is never to be thought of as something fixed and static, externally given and imposed. Rather it is something which needs to be constantly rediscovered, which has its own internal dynamism, and which is indeed re-asserting itself in our own time. For if on the one hand the age in which we live often seems blind to spiritual realities, we must also acknowledge that it is an age which has seen an amazing rediscovery of unity amongst the Christian people, a rediscovery which has manifested itself less at the level of organisation — at this level the ecumenical movement has known many set-backs — than at the level of a rediscovered unity and fullness of vision. All that is written in these pages is in some sense a product of that ecumenical discovery. It is written from within a particular way of receiving and holding the Christian faith, the tradition of the Church of England, but it is written from the experience of a constant interaction and exchange with other traditions, an interaction which for the writer goes back to the first beginnings of his attempts to reflect upon his faith. 'We go out to learn from the stranger. We return to find ourselves enriched at home.' If that is true of our meetings with men of other faiths it is certainly true of our meetings with our fellow-Christians of other traditions. Indeed it may well be the development of this inter-Christian dialogue which has made possible the first openings of this wider exchange.

Much is spoken in these pages of tradition. Tradition itself speaks of that which is received and handed on. We have nothing which was not given us.

I am a debtor to all, to all I am bounden,

writes Edwin Muir, one of the true seers of our time; and in another poem written in the last days of his life:

I have been taught by dreams and fantasies
Learned from the friendly and the darker phantoms
And got great knowledge and courtesy from the dead
Kinsmen and kinswomen, ancestors and friends
But from two mainly
Who gave me birth. '

If there are many quotations in this book, it is not only on account of the writer's poverty of invention, though that certainly has something to do with it. It is meant as a way of expressing that indebtedness to the dead kinsmen and kinswomen, the sense that 'nothing that exists is an island unto itself.' [6] It also says something about the nature of that tradition which is not only a handing on of a heritage through time, but also the handing over of a gift from eternity to time. 'For it is not you who speak, but the Spirit of your Father who speaketh in you' (Matt. 10:20). Who can speak of the things of God, but the Spirit who searches the deep things of God? So in the words of a sixth-century Patriarch of Jerusalem, of a nineteenth-century farmer's daughter in Wales, of a seventeenth-century scholar in England, of a twentieth-century monk in Kentucky, so in the life of one of the greatest saints of the Russian East, we catch some echo of the words of God. These are witnesses who speak together in concordant testimony, even though the Churches

to which they belonged excommunicated and ignored one another.
Where men were making discord, the divine grace, which always
heals what is wounded and makes up what is lacking, was creating
unity. And the tradition is not a thing of the past. The Spirit speaks
now, so that his words may find a place in us as they did in them, so
that in our world there may continue to be both an *incarnatio Dei*
and an *inspiratio hominis*, in the meeting of man's freedom with the
wholly unlooked-for gift and act of God.

As is suggested in the last two pieces in this book, this enlivening
of the tradition can sometimes take place when we become able to
hear the prophetic voices of some of the poets and writers of our
day. We have already cited Edwin Muir. It is enough to mention
the names of David Jones and T. S. Eliot to reveal more of the
richness of this line of enquiry. Here are men whose writing em-
bodies that awareness of tradition of which we have spoken, who in
their different ways present us with a vision of the world as full of
God's glory. The message which such men convey need not always
be so consciously conceived. In his humility Muir doubted whether
his great poem on the Transfiguration was Christian at all. It was
only after it was published that he became aware of the Orthodox
understanding of the transfiguration of the world. David Jones,
whose understanding of his art was much more explicitly theological
than Edwin Muir's seems yet not to have realised the full implications of what he was saying in the strictly theological sphere. There
is much here for further reflection, hitherto unexploited resources for
the development of a practical and healing understanding of the
faith, for a new realisation of the implications of the intersection of
the timeless with time.

To speak of spirituality is to speak of that meeting of eternity
with time, of heaven with earth; it is to recover a sense of the
holiness of matter, the sacredness of this world of space and time
when it is known as the place of God's epiphany. Above all it is to
 know that man's life, man's body, is to be the place of God. There is
a geography of the holy places, the places where the saints have
dwelt, Oxford and Athos, Canterbury and Cernica, St Davids and
Zagorsk; places whose beauty has been revealed by lives which have
been open to God in such a way as to show that this world is not a
system closed upon itself. These are places whose power persists

through centuries of indifference and neglect to be revealed again when men are ready for it, places which display the potential holiness of all this earth which man has loved so much, yet so much ravaged.

One such place is to be found at the furthest tip of Brittany, Landevennec, in the early period of the Celtic Church a great centre of light and learning, then for long centuries in eclipse, finally destroyed at the time of the French revolution only to come to new life within our own generation. The monastery is placed as many monasteries are, in a situation of outstanding natural beauty. On the shores of an estuary, sheltered from the storms of the Atlantic it enjoys what we should call a 'micro-climate'. Wrdisten, the writer of the earliest life of its founder St Guenolé, puts the matter more simply. 'The spring flowers make their earliest appearance there and the autumn leaves linger there longer than anywhere else. It is a kind of Paradise prepared by God for his servants, and, as it is rich in the fruits of the earth, so it is rich in heavenly fruits.' [7] The writer tells us how at the beginning of the community's life in the time of the founder, it was discovered that none of the monks could die, even though they suffered the infirmities of old age. 'The oldest of the brethren, burdened by the weight of many years longed to be dissolved and released from this crumbling frame of clay.' The reason why this was so was finally revealed. In a vision the brethren saw an opening in heaven above the monastery exactly the size of the monastery itself, and the angels of God ascending and descending. The correspondence of earth and heaven, of time and eternity was so exact, that here on earth time seemed to have come to a stop. The brethren exhorted their abbot to pull down the buildings and to move a little nearer to the shore. And this they did. Even this slight removal secured the desired effect. It became possible to die, but only from old age; and for a long time the writer assures us that the brethren died only in strict order of seniority. 'And this was long the rule in the monastery and has only recently been changed.'

Out of the turbulence of the little tribal kingdoms of Celtic Wales and Brittany where life was precarious and short, where violence reigned, there comes the story of serenity and peace, speaking to us in poetic language of the possibility that here in this world of flesh and blood men can realise, if only for an instant, the presence of the kingdom of eternity which is ever at hand, can recapture the innocence of the beginning and anticipate the fulfilment of the end. Heaven and earth are linked in a single bond, and the world is a wedding; the angels of God ascend and descend upon the sons of men. Such a moment cannot last. The two spheres may even come too close together. It is not possible to maintain the original vision in all its brilliance. We have to return to the limitations of our lot. But in such an instant of vision, arising like the icons of Rublev from the cruelty and strife of human history, we glimpse something of the unmeasured possibilities of human life and its unfathomable mystery when it is lived in the growing realisation of the presence and power of God.

NOTES

1. R. W. Church, *Pascal and Other Sermons* (London 1896) p. 82.
2. John Keble, *Sermons Academical and Occasional* (Oxford 1847) p. 356.
3. David Jenkins, *The Contradiction of Christianity* (London 1976) p. 88.
4. Thomas McFarland, *Coleridge and the Pantheist Tradition* (Oxford 1969) p 161.
5. Edwin Muir, *Collected Poems* (London 1960) p. 302.
6. Nathan Scott, *Negative Capability* (Yale 1969) p. 99.
7. Gilbert H. Doble, *The Saints of Cornwall*, part II (Oxford 1962) p. 70 and p. 75. The Section on St Winwaloe (Guenolé) is from pp. 59–108.

I

IN FLESH AND IN SPIRIT

1

Tradition and life

spirituality and the new consciousness

To speak of 'the new consciousness' in connection with the tradition of Christian spirituality is already to speak of relating the present to the past. But I would maintain that this relationship is to be expressed in a tradition which is alive, which grows and changes in response to the demands of the times which we live in. And this spirituality with which we are concerned is never to be abstract, disembodied spirituality. It is, in the words of one of the very first Christian writers, 'in flesh and in Spirit', in deed and in truth.

I should like to begin with a number of stories, for as I understand it, the new consciousness, like the old spirituality in this, prefers to express itself by way of anecdote and image rather than by purely rational discourse.

And first, an Hasidic story, familiar to many and handed down in various versions, of a poor Rabbi in Cracow who dreamed that there was a great treasure buried under the bridge in front of the royal palace in Prague. He set out for Prague to see whether he could acquire this treasure. When he got there he found, naturally enough, that the bridge was very carefully guarded. After some days of loitering and speculating, he was drawn into conversation with one of the palace guards, and found himself admitting that he had dreamed that there was treasure there. 'Why,' the guard exclaimed, 'you are a fool! Only last night I dreamed about a Rabbi in Cracow, looking very much like you, who had treasure buried in his backyard. But you don't think I'd be fool enough to set off for Cracow in search of it.' [1]

We have treasure in the backyard. But we shall not find it unless we are prepared to go on a lengthy journey, and to learn about it from a stranger.

Secondly, there is the famous conversation between St Francis and Brother Leo on the subject of perfect joy. We recall how St Francis says that if when we come to the friary, cold and tired and wet through, the brothers reject us and won't let us in, but rather drive us away as impostors, but 'if with patience and gladness we suffer all these things thinking on the pains of the blessed Christ, then, Brother Leo, write that here is perfect joy.'[2] Less well known is an incident in the life of a Sufi saint in the ninth century of our era, Ibrahim ben Adham. 'On one occasion he arrived at a village in pouring rain, with his patched robe soaked through and his body chilled by the bitter cold. He went to a mosque, but was refused admittance, and at three others he failed to find shelter. Then in despair he entered a bath-house and sat close to the stove, the smoke from which blackened his face and his clothes. Then he knew complete satisfaction.'[3]

The way which leads to the perfect joy which comes from the knowledge and the love of God is one which goes by the way of extreme paradox. We find the fullness of God at the moment of man's greatest emptiness.

My third story comes from nearer our own time and place, from Zürich in the winter of 1934. 'I had gone', Gerhard Adler tells us, 'to one of the by now almost legendary seminars which Jung used to give on Wednesday mornings. . . .' This particular seminar was on the interpretation of visions and had been running for four years. On this morning, Adler says, 'it had been one of those days when Jung had been at his very best and had talked out of his profoundest depth and immediacy, which is to say he had communicated a great deal of his unique wisdom and knowledge. . . . I had felt deeply touched and stirred by all that had been said. With me that morning there had been two close friends; together we left the house in the Gemeindestrasse in silence and concentration. I was the first to break the silence, saying, "Today he has truly talked about myself and my crucial problems, and answered all my unasked questions." I shall never forget the almost indignant protest with which first the one then the other friend interrupted me. "But *no*, he talked about

my problems." "Nonsense, it was exactly my questions he
answered." We broke off and looked at each other, realising that a
man had talked to us out of the centre of his being, and therefore
from such a level that he had included all our individual personalities
and transcended them, that here we had been in the presence of, and
touched by, a human commitment of a completeness and intensity,
such as only men of true genius are capable of producing.' [4]

When we reach a certain depth of human life and experience, a
certain depth of holiness, we find that our existence as persons is
very different from our existence as individuals. There is an inter-
dependence and an interpenetration of such a nature as to allow us
to say that in God, all men are one man, one man is all men. If we
are to rediscover this in reality and experience, not only as an attrac-
tive theory, we shall have much to learn from modern psychiatry,
not least from the school of C. G. Jung.

We have begun with three stories. All of them take us to the frontiers of the Christian tradition with which we are familiar. They
take us to areas fashionable enough, in a superficial way, today, but
very little regarded by Christians even thirty or forty years ago, to
the tradition of the Hasidim within Judaism, of the Sufis within
Islam and to the explorations of contemporary psychiatry. All of
them take us to the edge of our tradition and then send us back to its
centre to rediscover meanings and realities which lie at its heart. All
of them, in different ways, throw light on the new consciousness
which has been coming to birth within our Western European –
North American world of thought and understanding in this last
generation. Let us consider three basic points.

1. The world is one world. It is the stalest of platitudes. But it is
evidently true not only at the level of technology and scientific ad-
vance; it is true in a more mysterious way at the level of man's innermost search for life and value. We go out to learn from the
stranger. We return to find ourselves enriched at home. We can see
the pattern at work in the lives of many of the greatest Christian
figures of our century. Louis Massignon, the outstanding French
Islamic scholar, did not become less a Christian than most of his
academic contemporaries, on account of his conviction that he owed
his faith and his life to the prayers of his Muslim friends. On the
contrary, in him a lifetime of the service and study of Islam and

Christianity so penetrated and were at one that at the time of his death a Muslim friend could describe him as 'the most Muslim of Christians, the most Christian of Muslims'. The same would be true of two other Frenchmen, Jules Monchanin and Henri Le Saux, in relation to their meeting with Hinduism. His deep and living initiation into the Hindu way of prayer and faith did not make Henri Le Saux, Swami Abhishiktananda as he became, less a Christian than he was before. Rather in the life and teachings of such a man we begin to glimpse something of the dimensions of the mystery of God revealed in Christ, begin indeed to learn a little of what it could mean in our own century to be a Christian. We begin to see how much greater that mystery is than our comprehension of it, how its operations are at work far beyond the historical embodiment of it in what we have called Christendom.

The same process can be seen at work in our English-speaking world. We may think of Thomas Merton and his life-giving encounter with Zen. In England we may think of the work of Kenneth Cragg in relation to Islam, or the significance of the encounter with African religions for a man such as John Taylor, Bishop of Winchester.[5] And this encounter with another religious tradition, this rediscovery of the Christian faith which proceeds from it, something which even fifty years ago was a fairly rare and hazardous exploit, has now become something relatively common.

2. This new encounter with the reality of other faiths already tells us something vital about the 'old consciousness' which has so rapidly been collapsing in these last decades and of the 'new consciousness' which grows out of this collapse. What has suddenly disappeared is a way of thought and experience, which is old in terms of American history, since it came to birth in the sixteenth and seventeenth centuries, but which is relatively young in terms of our European tradition, though we often forget this fact. This was the consciousness of renaissance and reformation man, above all of the man of the philosophical and scientific revolution of the seventeenth century. It was a consciousness confident, aggressive, analytical, utilitarian, which allowed no questioning of the absolute superiority of the Western way of life over all other civilisations. It affected, much more deeply than we knew, the underlying attitudes of all our Western traditions of Christianity. It has carried this way of life all

over the globe and as far as the moon, and at the moment of its greatest triumph it has suddenly lost confidence in itself. This loss of confidence takes innumerable forms. We can see it, for instance, in the world of education and the churches, in our humiliating inability to hand on the tradition which we have received. We have found that the younger members of our society are often no longer interested in receiving it, at least in the form in which it is presented to them. They have carried out a kind of internal emigration.

This loss of confidence has happened fairly recently. Less than forty years ago it was axiomatic to most Englishmen and most Americans that they had nothing to learn from Muslims and Jews, still less from Hindus and Buddhists. Even our fellow-Christians of the East, who had to some extent escaped the influence both of renaissance and reformation, seemed a remarkably unimpressive lot. The Eastern Churches, Bishop Hensley Henson remarks, in his elegant prose, 'have sunk into an almost barbaric superstition . . . isolated from the progressive influences which have created the civilisation of the West, and, subjected to the harsh dominance of a culture inferior morally and intellectually to their own, they have acquired the distinctive vices of the oppressed, suspicion, servility and deceit.'[6] The years which have passed since those words were published in 1939 have taught us a little too much of the distinctive vices of the oppressor, arrogance, cruelty and deceit, to make us feel happy with the calmly superior tone of the Bishop of Durham. The blows which our civilisation has received and is receiving, from without and from within, leave us in no doubt that something is terrifyingly wrong, that we are in need of a wisdom and balance which our tradition, in its currently received form, seems unable to give us. We have a strong suspicion that we must look for the indications of the way forward in precisely those places where our predecessors would least have thought to look for it; in the other ancient traditions of prayer and wisdom, and among the despised, the oppressed, the unheard minorities.

In particular, of course, Western man's confidence in himself has been undermined by the revelation of the depths of destructive evil and irrationality which have opened up in the heart of his seemingly rational and progressive world. We may think of the concentration camps of Nazi Germany, of the Gulag Archipelago of Soviet

Russia, of other less blatant forms of evil uncomfortably nearer home. There is the possibility of an appalling horror which lurks in the midst of our human life, which we have to live with and if possible understand. We are indebted to those like Bruno Bettelheim, in one way, or Alexander Solzhenitsyn in another, who begin to help us to remember, and even maybe to make a healing *anamnesis* of things which it is very difficult to bring to mind, things of which we may well say 'the remembrance of them is grievous unto us, the burden of them is intolerable.' If the 'new consciousness' of which we speak is to be more than a passing fashion, it must learn to assimilate something of the meaning of this experience of darkness; that is to say something about death, the Cross, the descent into hell.

The life of St Francis, of course, points us to this. It is a joyful life, not a comfortable one. If Francis possesses the world, it is because he has stripped himself of everything. If he knows the fullness of joy he has found it through the uttermost of pain and suffering. And it is evident that this pattern of life through death, which is at the heart of the Christian mystery, and of which we are inclined to speak too easily, is the pattern which is to be found everywhere on the way to God. We see it in the story of Ibrahim ben Adham, the Sufi saint; we find it in the *koan* of Zen Buddhism. The way through into hope lies beyond hope; the way through into knowledge beyond what we usually call knowledge. In the massive testimony of a Solzhenitsyn we see again how out of defeat and utmost degradation men can find in God new hope and new life. The uniqueness of Christ's death and resurrection, of his conquest over death by death is evidently an inclusive not an exclusive thing.

The new consciousness can take our secure and comfortable Western man and cast him down in the dust, in flesh and in spirit. He finds himself like Dom Le Saux 'on the ground pressing with fervent hands the feet of the master', in this case an outwardly unremarkable Indian guru;[7] or like the young Englishman who recently published an account of the spiritual pilgrimage which brought him back to be confirmed in the Church of England, walking across India begging his food from the villagers he met.[8] The way forward may be surprisingly narrow, the gate low.

3. But through this narrow way, there is a road which goes on. By way of the death which leads into life we find ourselves in a

large room. Through this confrontation with evil, and after this descent into hell, man is able to receive the Spirit, and in the Spirit he
finds that he is reconciled and at one with his body and the senses,
with his unconscious as well as his conscious, with his neighbour and
with the world. Suddenly a new possibility of wholeness appears
in human life. He begins to discover the scope of the inward
dimensions of the human person, the potential catholicity of each
one. In each one of us all are present when we stand before God in
prayer. What Gerhard Adler speaks about in relation to Jung,
Merton describes, certainly on the basis of his own experience, but
in terms suggested by the work of Reza Arasted, a Persian psychiatrist versed in the tradition of the Sufis:

'The man who has attained final integration is no longer limited
by the culture in which he has grown up. He has embraced all
life. . . . He has experienced qualities of every type of life. . . . He
does not remain bound to one limited set of values in such a way
that he opposes them aggressively or defensively to others. He is fully "Catholic" in the best sense of the word. He has a unified vision
and experience of the one truth shining out in all its various
manifestations, some clearer than others, some more definite and
certain than others. He does not set these partial views up in opposition to one another, but unifies them in a dialectic or in-sight of
complementarity. With this view of life he is able to bring perspective, liberty and spontaneity into the lives of others.'[9] There opens
up in the growth of the new consciousness, an awareness of the
wholeness of man's life and being.

It would be easy at this point to make a fatal misunderstanding.
This catholicity, this comprehensiveness of which Merton speaks,
and which he himself knew in practice, is not to be reached by any
superficial kind of syncretism, by a simple combining of a little of
this tradition with a little of that, so as to create a kind of home-
made patchwork. Let us take another quotation from Merton, about
the encounter of the religions, taken from a lecture written in the last
months of his life. 'This contemplative dialogue must be reserved for
those who have entered . . . with full seriousness into their own
tradition, and are in authentic contact with the past of their own
religious community – besides being open to the tradition and the
heritage of experience belonging to other communities.' [10] We must,

if we are to do anything of value in this field, <u>know our own</u> <u>heritage, be in touch with our own roots.</u>

This brings us back sharply to our own backyard. Is this where the treasure is to be found? As a small black boy said to me some years ago as he came in through the entrance of the General Theological Seminary in New York, 'Is this the cemetery, Mister?' Is such a place the place of death, or of death and resurrection? What is the tradition to which we belong? Has it any particular significance in terms of the dilemmas of the present moment?

In fact the four figures who are to be found on the seal of the General Theological Seminary surrounding the central figure of the Lord, are St Athanasius, St Gregory Nazianzen, St Ambrose and St Augustine.[11] Looking out with mild surprise onto the traffic in Ninth Avenue they suggest to me that whatever the tradition is by which we live, it is not exactly the tradition of renaissance and reformation man. I have written of the collapse of our public Western tradition; we are all aware of it. But I have also hinted that there may be strands within it which have been neglected or overlaid, which are full of promise for the future. That there are such strands I am convinced, and I believe that we as Anglicans have a particular part to play in their recovery. We are called to embody in the English-speaking world a certain vision of the wholeness and balance, the Catholicity of the Christian tradition. We are called to witness to the sacramental quality of all things through the specifically sacramental nature of our life together. And in some special way we are called to remind the West of the almost forgotten world of the Christian East, of the heritage and experience of the fathers of the Church.

It would of course be absurd to suggest that we can do these things by ourselves alone. Ours is one tradition among many, and we must be prepared at all times to work in collaboration with all our fellow-Christians who are aware of the same calling. But nonetheless our history places upon us a special opportunity and a special obligation.

What does this obligation involve? I would begin with a quotation from one of the greatest Anglican theologians of the nineteenth century. '<u>All Christian life is sacramental</u>. Not alone in our highest act of Communion are we partaking of heavenly powers through earthly signs and vehicles. This neglected faith may be revived through increased sympathy with the earth derived from fuller knowledge, through a fearless love of all things.' [12] The words are Hort's. They speak of a vision of the world as sacrament, a vision of the world as full of the operations of the divine glory. It is a vision which is not afraid of the goodness and beauty of the material order, but which believes that God is to be known and loved in and through the things which he has made, and that those things are to be known and loved in him. It is a vision which has its roots in the greatest spokesman of our tradition since the Reformation, Richard Hooker.

'God hath his influence into the very essence of all things, without which influence of Deity supporting them their utter annihilation could not but follow. Of him all things have both received their first being and their continuance, to be that which they are. All things are therefore partakers of God, they are his offspring, his influence is in them, and the personal wisdom of God is for that very cause said to excel in nimbleness or agility, to pierce into all intellectual pure and subtile spirits, to go through all and to reach unto everything that is. . . . So that all things which God hath made are in that respect the offspring of God, they are in him as effects in their highest cause, he likewise is actually in them, the assistance and influence of his Deity is their life.' [13] This presence of God in his world is experienced and known by men in a great variety of ways, not only in actions which we are accustomed to call religious. 'We move, we sleep, we take the cup at the hand of our friend, a number of things we often times do, only to satisfy some natural desire, without present, express and actual reference unto any commandment of God. Unto his glory even these things are done which we naturally perform, and not only that which morally and spiritually we do. For by every effect proceeding from the most concealed instincts of nature his power is made manifest.' [14]

It is frequently said at the present time, that our Western Christianity, in particular in its Reformation forms, has suffered from a doctrine of the divine transcendence which has cut creation off from a real participation in the life of God, and which has restricted God to a progressively narrower area of man's 'moral and spiritual' life. There is, I believe, truth in this observation. But it is evidently not true of the tradition which stems from Richard Hooker. There it is clear that already in the act of creation there is a co-inherence of God with all that he has made. It is said moreover that this Reformation tradition has signally failed to include man's body in its vision of our approach to God, that it has been unable to hold together heart and head, feeling and understanding in any unified or integrated approach to divine things. This too is surely true in many ways, though as I shall suggest in more detail later, it is notably untrue of the tradition which we inherit. It was precisely on such points as these, the use of the ring in marriage, of the sign of the cross in baptism, of bodily gesture in approaching God's altar, that the seventeenth-century controversies took place. In themselves, the issues seem small ones. Taken together they have great significance.

To look to the United States, the form of Christian faith and life which was implanted in New England by the Founding Fathers, and which has had so deep an influence on the whole subsequent development of American religion and culture, decisively rejected such bodily actions. If a foreigner may be permitted a large generalisation, it seems as if in the whole American religious tradition there has been a particular difficulty in holding together heart and head, piety and theology, enthusiasm and reflection; and this has come from a lack of understanding of the role of sacramental symbols. There is a tendency to oscillate between forms of Christian life which are intellectual and dry on the one side, and ones that are fervent but lacking in critical discernment, on the other.

Here again the opposed position of our Anglican tradition is of the greatest importance. The figure of the American Dr Samuel Johnson, the outstanding theologian of our Church in the colonial period is crucial here. D. F. Gerardi in his study of his thought sees it as an attempt to find a middle ground between the enthusiasm of the Great Awakening on one side, and the rational liberalism of the American Enlightenment on the other, an effort to fuse the heart and mind of religious experience.[15] This, which Calvinism had failed to do in one way, and which the Enlightenment failed to do in another, Johnson sought to achieve in terms of 'the sacramental piety' of the Anglican tradition. It is indeed fascinating to find in a man so much a part of his age as Samuel Johnson of Connecticut, a defence of the body's place in Christian worship. 'Significant actions are as properly language as articulate sounds, so that there is really no more reason to object against this kind of language than any other that is used in our service. . . . The eye is apt to affect the heart and the liveliness and activity of our bodies naturally awakens and enlivens our minds. . . .' We find too, in this context, a statement of the social implications of the practice of common prayer, and a grounding of it all in the doctrine of the incarnation. 'By dwelling in the tabernacle of his body, he has united himself to and dwells in mankind, especially in the faithfull, who are made members of his body by Baptism, and are partakers of his blessed Body and Blood in the Holy Eucharist.' [16]

Here in this splendid statement of the meaning of the incarnation, in which it is said that God the Word 'has united himself to and dwells in mankind, especially in the faithful,' we have the theological principle which allows us to see the activity of the Word in men of all faiths, without losing the inclusive centrality and uniqueness of Christ. Without such a vision of the meaning of the incarnation, we shall find ourselves either refusing to see the activity of God in the other traditions, or sacrificing the essential Christian affirmation of the centrality of Christ. With it, the tradition can unfold from within, without betraying its essential character. We have also, by implication, in such a view a way of seeing the sacramental quality of all creation, and hence the roots of an answer to the problems of the environment which have become so urgent to us today.

Here is the traditional Anglican theology of the incarnation, with its sacramental consequences direct and indirect, and it is not a theology which is in any way an alternative to, or substitute for a religion of redemption through the sacrifice of the Cross, or a religion of the coming of the Spirit at Pentecost to renew the face of the earth. Rather it lays the foundation on which these further stages of the divine economy may be based. The tendency to set one thing over against another thing, rather than to allow the different elements of doctrine and practice to balance and complement one another, is something which our tradition has sought to avoid since the end of the sixteenth century. The writing of Samuel Johnson of

Connecticut is in this respect simply a continuation of the great tradition inaugurated one hundred and fifty years earlier by men like Richard Hooker and Lancelot Andrewes, the two teachers who hold a position of unrivalled authority in the development of our tradition. And Lancelot Andrewes is not only the preacher of sermons for Christmas; nor even for Good Friday and Easter. He is also the preacher of Pentecost, and few theologians demonstrate so clearly both the coherence and balance of Christian doctrine, and the way in which the doctrine of the Holy Spirit comes as the crown and fulfilment of the whole scheme.

In any attempt to grasp the Christian tradition of spirituality it is clear that the doctrine of the Holy Spirit is of crucial importance. For in this context the word itself must refer, not to any created spirit, human or other, but to man's life in the Holy Spirit, and to the gifts and workings of the Holy Spirit in the hearts and minds of men. In the presence of the Holy Spirit we see that tradition, far from being a merely historical maintenance of a teaching or structure externally received, is the ever new imparting of an inward gift of life and knowledge, of insight and experience. The historical line of handing on from generation to generation is constantly enlivened by the descent of the Spirit who is the Lord and giver of life. The epiclesis of the Holy Spirit, which since the end of the eighteenth century has never been absent from the Eucharistic heart of the Episcopal Church, gives us a clue to the nature of the Church's life as a whole.

We have much to learn of all this from the Whitsun sermons of Lancelot Andrewes. 'Howsoever we make it, sure it is that all the rest, all the feasts hitherto in the return of the year from his incarnation to the very last of his ascension, though all of them be great and worthy of all honour in themselves, yet to us they are as nothing, any of them or all of them, even all the feasts in the calendar without this day, this feast which now we hold holy to the sending of the Holy Ghost.' Without his coming, Christ the Word is 'but words spoken or words written'; it is in the coming of the Spirit that there is the actual possession of what is promised in Christ. Both advents are necessary and complement each other.

'These, if we should compare them, it would not be easy to determine, whether is the greater of the two: 1. That of the Prophet,

Filius datus est nobis; 2. or that of the Apostle, *Spiritus datus est nobis*, the ascending of our flesh, or the descending of his Spirit; *incarnatio Dei* or *inspiratio hominis*; the mystery of his incarnation or the mystery of our inspiration. For mysteries they are both, and "great mysteries of godliness" both. . . . But we will not compare them, they are both above all comparison. Yet this we may safely say of them; without either of them we are not complete, we have not our accomplishment; but by both we have, and that fully, even by this day's royal exchange. Whereby as before he of ours, so now we of his are made partakers. He clothed with our flesh and we invested with his Spirit. The great promise of the Old Testament accomplished, that he should partake our human nature; and the great and precious promise of the New, that we should be *consortes divinae naturae*, "partakers of his divine nature", both are this day accomplished.'[17]

Here indeed is a royal exchange in this *incarnatio Dei* and this *inspiratio hominis*, this taking of man's flesh into God, this breathing of God's Spirit into man. Here is the fullness of that vision and experience by which the Church lived in the first ten centuries of its history, that interchange of God with man so wonderfully articulated in the theology of a Maximus the Confessor. We have here the heart of what we could mean by spirituality in the Christian sense of the word: God's lifting up of man in his fullness to share in the very eternity of his life, God's entering into man in his fullness 'by the communion of his blessed Spirit'; and this not as a thing which has happened in the past, but as a mystery which is all around us and within us in the present. For if the *incarnatio Dei* is rooted in the once-for-all act of God in Christ, the *inspiratio hominis*, the union of man with God, by God's breathing of his life into us, is a thing of this very moment, of this place, of this flesh and of this blood. And, as Andrewes assures us, the one mystery is as great as the other, the one is not complete without the other.

It is as we begin to realise this fact 'in flesh and in Spirit' that we shall have the foundation of what will truly be a new consciousness, new with the eternal creativity of God himself, not with the newness of some passing human fashion, a new consciousness in the Spirit, when as St Gregory of Nyssa says, we shall see with the eyes of the Dove; when with St Paul we shall be able to declare, 'We have the mind of Christ.'

NOTES

1. I owe this story to my friend Donald Nicholl. Anyone who knows his tract *Scientia Cordis* will see the similarities of our approach.

2. St Francis of Assisi, *The Legends and Lauds*, ed. Otto Karrer (1947) p. 186.

3. Margaret Smith, *The Way of the Mystics* (1976) p. 182.

4. Gerhard Adler in *Harvest, The Journal for Jungian Studies of the Analytical Psychology Club*, London, Number 21 (1975) p. 1.

5. Cf. Kenneth Cragg's numerous writings on Islam, and Bishop John Taylor's book, *The Primal Vision*.

6. H. Hensley Henson, *The Church of England* (1939) pp. 240–1.

7. See Abhishiktananda, *Guru and Disciple, passim.*

8. Roger van de Weyer, *Guru Jesus* (1976).

9. Thomas Merton, *Contemplation in a World of Action* (1972) p. 212.

10. Thomas Merton, *The Asian Journal* (1974) p. 316.

11. The seal in its present form dates from the reforms of Dean Hoffman in the 1880s. P. M. Dawley, *The Story of the General Theological Seminary* (1969) p. 265.

12. F. J. A. Hort, *The Way, the Truth and the Life* p. 213.

13. Richard Hooker, *Laws of Ecclesiastical Polity*, V. 56.5.

14. *ibid.* V. 48.2.

15. See D. F. Gerardi, *The American Doctor Johnson: Anglican Piety and the 18th Century Mind* (unpublished doctoral dissertation, Columbia. 1971).

16. See Louis Weil, *Worship and Sacraments in the Teaching of Samuel Johnson of Connecticut* (unpublished doctoral thesis at the Institut Catholique, Paris) p. 118 and p. 153.

17. Lancelot Andrewes, *Complete Works* (Library of Anglo-Catholic Theology) Vol III pp. 108–9.

Two Worlds in One:

the transformation of the senses

In the last chapter, I wrote in general terms of the nature of the new consciousness which seems to be coming to birth in us and around us, and of some of the elements in the tradition of Christian spirituality – often despised and neglected elements – which seem to respond to its demands. Now we shall concentrate on one particular topic, the place of the senses, sight and hearing, taste and touch and smell, in our approach to God. Is there only one world, the one which we perceive every day, or are there in reality two worlds, this and the world beyond, and if there are indeed two, how are they connected with each other?

I shall begin with a statement of one of the great poets of our century:

So from the ground we felt that virtue branch
Through all our veins till we were whole, our wrists
As fresh and pure as water from a well,
Our hands made new to handle holy things,
The source of all our seeing rinsed and cleansed
Till earth and light and water entering there
Gave back to us the clear unfallen world.
We could have thrown our clothes away for lightness,
But that even they, though sour and travel stained,
Seemed, like our flesh, made of immortal substance,
And the soiled flax and wool lay light upon us
Like friendly wonders, flower and flock entwined

As in a morning field. Was it a vision?
Or did we see that day the unseeable
One glory of the everlasting world
Perpetually at work, though never seen
Since Eden locked the gate that's everywhere
And nowhere? Was the change in us alone,
And the enormous earth still left forlorn,
An exile or a prisoner? . . .

And this is not only a vision of the world of nature restored. This
light brings healing and freedom to the world of men.

The shepherd's hovels shone, for underneath
The soot we saw the stone clean at the heart
As on the starting-day. The refuse heaps
Were grained with that fine dust that made the world;
For he had said, 'To the pure all things are pure.'
And when we went into the town, he with us,
The lurkers under doorways, murderers,
With rags tied round their feet for silence, came
Out of themselves to us and were with us,
And those who hide within the labyrinth
Of their own loneliness and greatness, came,
And those entangled in their own devices,
The silent and the garrulous liars, all
Stepped out of their dungeons and were free. [1]

The poem from which I have quoted came to Edwin Muir out of
certain visionary experiences which he had during analysis. He
called it from the first 'The Transfiguration', though he seems to
have been doubtful how Christian it was, since it was not so much
about the transfiguration of Christ, as about the transfiguration of
the world in the presence of Christ. It was only after its publication
that he discovered that this understanding of the Transfiguration as
including the whole creation was an essential element of the Eastern
Orthodox teaching on the subject.

In the poem Muir asks, was it illusion or truth? Was the change
in us, or in the world? Is such a moment of vision a passing decep-

tion, or does it disclose the underlying, the eternal nature of things?

If we go back into Christian tradition we should need to go to the later period of the Byzantine Empire to find the fullest and most clearly articulated answer to these questions. It was the age of St Gregory Palamas and Nicholas Cabasilas, an age which placed the mystery of our Lord's Transfiguration at the very centre of its understanding of God, man's nature and the world. It was an age which affirmed that while God in himself, in his essence, is wholly beyond the reach of our faculties, yet in his operations, the energies of his glory, he truly makes himself known even to our senses. Through the activity of the Holy Spirit in the lives of men and women, the heart and its perceptions are so cleansed that we may see with our bodily eyes, 'the unseeable/One glory of the everlasting world,/Perpetually at work though never seen,/since Eden locked the gate that's everywhere/And nowhere.'

This faith and vision which was focussed in the person of the Lord Christ on the mountain of the Transfiguration, was, for that age, renewed in the living experience of the Church, an experience which itself was focussed on the Holy Mountain of Athos, in the communities and hermitages of the monastic republic. From that central point the light flooded out into the whole surrounding world. Its radiance survived the collapse of the Byzantine Empire; we see it reflected in the painted monasteries of Northern Romania in the sixteenth and seventeenth centuries; we find it again in the spirituality of nineteenth-century Russia, in the life of a St Seraphim of Sarov, in the writings of the unknown author of *The Way of a Pilgrim*. 'The prayer of my heart gave me such consolation that I felt there was no happier person on earth than I, and I doubted if there could be a greater and fuller happiness in the Kingdom of Heaven. Not only did I feel this in my own soul, but the whole outside world also seemed to me to be full of beauty and delight. Everything drew me to love and to thank God; people, trees, plants, animals. I saw them all as my kinsfolk. I found on them all the magic of the Name of Jesus.' [2] By the transformation of the heart, through the realisation of God's presence there at the centre of man's being, it becomes possible to see that 'heaven and earth are full of God's glory'. We discover our kinship with the material creation, we see all things marked with the name of Jesus. Here are two worlds, but two worlds in one; the familiar reality of earth shot through with the eternal reality of heaven.

Within Anglicanism we are sometimes conscious of this heritage of Eastern Orthodoxy and truly begin to feel it is a part of our own heritage. There is certainly at present a growing interest in the Eastern Christian tradition of theology and spirituality. But we should be very blind if we did not recognise that to the vast majority of our fellow-Christians in the West, the Orthodox tradition still appears to be something remote, irrelevant and inaccessible. Indeed in many ways it still is inaccessible; there is much still to be done to make the basic texts available in English, with commentaries which will show their actuality for our own day.

But this vision of a transfigured world which lies at the heart of Eastern Orthodoxy, and is articulated there with such power and such precision, is not absent from our own tradition in the West. If we look for it, we shall find this vision of the divine glory seen in and through the things of earth present in our own Anglican seventeenth century, in preachers and poets alike. In Thomas Traherne it reaches a memorable intensity of expression. 'By the very right of your senses, you enjoy the world' he tells us, and then goes on to expound what he means by this enjoyment of the world as God's word and gift to us. 'You never enjoy the world aright, till the sea itself floweth in your veins, till you are clothed with the heavens and crowned with the stars, and perceive yourself to be the sole heir of the whole world, and more than so, because others are in it who are everyone sole heirs, as well as you.' [3] It is typical of the general ignorance of our seventeenth-century heritage that a writer like Theodore Roszak in *Where the Wasteland Ends* can quote Traherne with great approval, evidently supposing him to be altogether untypical of his age. The eloquence of Traherne's poetic prose at its best is unsurpassed. The structure of his teaching, on the other hand, is representative of the tradition to which he belonged. The tone of sober ecstasy which marks so much of his writing could be found in others of his time, scholars as well as poets.

Here, as an example, is Mark Frank, writing on the power of joy to expand and integrate human life, bringing together body, mind and spirit in the renewal of the heart. 'Joy is the dilatation, the opening of the heart and sending out the spirits into all the parts. And if this joy we have, it will open our hearts to praise him; open our hearts to heaven to receive its influence; open our hearts to our needy brother to compassionate and relieve him; it will send out life and heat and spirit into all our powers — into our lips to sing unto him, into our fingers to play to him, into our feet even to leap for joy; into our eyes perpetually to gaze upon him; into our hands to open them for his sake plentifully to the poor; into the whole body to devote it wholly to his service.' [4] This is a rejoicing in God in which the body plays its part, a rejoicing which brings together what we should call social concerns, with a concern for man's inner life, which links outer and inner, head and heart. It would not be difficult to find other passages of a similar nature in Frank's sermons, nor to match them with places where he calls on the whole created world to aid mankind in praise of the Creator.

The seventeenth-century understanding of the correspondence between the inner world of man and the outer world of nature, the microcosm and the macrocosm, presupposed in such writings, was seriously undermined by the developments in science and philosophy which took place in the latter part of the seventeenth century. In a world dominated by the thought of Descartes and Locke, it became more and more difficult to see the bodily consequences of faith in the incarnation. But the vision was not entirely lost, and a large part of the aspiration of the English romantics, above all of Coleridge and Wordsworth, was towards its recovery. Here is a point where the Tractarians were very much the heirs of the Lake poets. They owed to them their renewed sense of the sacramental quality of all things, the context in which their renewed apprehension of the meaning of the particular sacraments of the Church is to be placed. They gained from Wordsworth in particular a sense of the holiness of the world, when it is known as God's world, the holiness of this material creation into which God has entered, in flesh.

One of the most remarkable of their early nineteenth-century forerunners perceived this clearly. Alexander Knox (1785–1831) writes, 'The Gospel commenced in an accommodation to man's animal exigencies which was as admirable as it was gracious. . . . The incarnation of the co-eternal Son, through which St John was enabled to declare what he and his fellow-Apostles had seen with

their eyes, what they "had looked upon, and their hands had handled, of the word of life", was in the first instance, so to consult
human nature in its animal and sensitive capacity, as to give the
strongest pledge that a dispensation thus introduced, would in every
subordinate provision, manifest the same spirit and operate on the
same principle.' ⁵ God's way of acting is all of a piece. The incarnation of the co-eternal Son is not an isolated wonder. 'The Word of
God, who is God, wills in all things to work the mystery of his incarnation.' The principle of sacrament and incarnation is to be seen
throughout. And in a strange way, when the human mind and intellect become particularly blind and deaf to the activities of God,
as in the last two centuries they undoubtedly have done, it seems as
though our salvation may come by way of the senses. Blake saw this
very clearly. But he was not alone. Others, in the nineteenth century
more centrally placed within the Christian tradition, had the same
perception. Commenting on Coleridge's interest in the pre-Socratic
philosophers, F. J. A. Hort remarks, 'Philosophy has denied that it
has anything to do with the knowledge of God, and is now being
rapidly swallowed up by positivism and science militant, and ancient experience tells us of a yet lower depth. Yet when we shall
seem to lie at the lowest point, we may perhaps be near the very
highest *and the senses themselves may become* the very instruments of
our deliverance.' ⁶ It is, I believe, one of the truly prophetic remarks
of the mid-nineteenth century.

Here in this comment on Coleridge's concern for the earliest
beginnings of Greek thought we meet with two of the primary
characteristics of the new consciousness of our own time. First, it is
aware of the threatened sacredness of the earth and of the body.
Secondly, it suspects that we Westerners have much to learn from
ancient and forgotten elements within our own tradition, and from
unknown or primitive peoples whom formerly we would have
despised. In many places, in the United States for instance, this discovery has been bound up with the exploration of minority groups
and movements of all kinds. One might think for instance of the
Shakers, in whose life and work and craftsmanship the principle of
the incarnation was worked out with wonderful thoroughness. Hear
Elder Frederick Evans on the subject of bread. 'I want something
solid and substantial. . . . I want to see the redemption of the

stomach, redemption of the land; and the redemption of the creative forces of men and women. The first step in the work of human redemption is to make and eat good bread.' [7] Through the unselfconscious honesty and excellence of their workmanship, the Shakers were enabled to make beds and chairs of such a quality, that, as Merton used to say, they reveal the *logos*, the innermost principle of the object concerned. It was very typical of the mind of Merton that he would explain the meaning of Maximus the Confessor by means of illustrations taken from Shaker furniture. There was, as he perceived, a profound and authentic spirituality in the things they made and used. Even now the places they created convey directly to the visitor the sense of a world full of peace and light.

But, in the United States, perhaps more important even than the rediscovery of such an unexpected monastic movement has been the rediscovery of the existence, the meaning and wisdom of other ethnic groups. There is the whole world of 'black theology'. Then there is also the recognition of the place of the people who were in that continent before the travellers from Europe arrived. I should suppose that this rediscovery of the American Indian heritage has had a double effect for those who have made it. On the one side there is the liberation which comes from acknowledging guilt for so nearly destroying their culture; on the other side there is the revelation of the content of that tradition, the powerful American Indian sense of the holiness of the earth and of man's kinship with the world of plants and animals, perceptions which speak particularly strongly to our alienated situation.

In Britain we have a similar situation, one which may seem remote from American experience, but which in reality is not so, since historically it lies behind the American dilemmas. We too have our American Indians. They are called the Welsh. The identification is not mine; it is that of a number of the leading figures in the Welsh national movement today, not least Dr Bobi Jones. It is an identification which, as yet, very few of the English have come to recognise. For fourteen hundred years we have trained ourselves not to notice the continued existence of the language and tradition of the people who were in the island of Britain before us, and who gave that island its name, Prydain Fawr. We have all been conditioned to consider the Welsh language and heritage as of no importance. The secrets of renewal are very close to us, around us and within us, so close to us indeed that we have often failed to notice them.

I have come to believe in the last fifteen years, in which I have gradually been coming to discover the existence of Wales, that our English inability to hear and learn Welsh, our unwillingness to acknowledge the existence of this language and this people, other than as an historical curiosity, is rooted in deep and unrecognised feelings of guilt dating back to the centuries of struggle during which our Anglo-Saxon ancestors conquered the greater part of Southern Britain and drove the earlier inhabitants back into the Western extremities of the island. Here we have the historical origins of some of the greatest weaknesses of our whole English-speaking world, weaknesses which all English-speaking peoples, despite the great diversity of their situations, to some extent, share. There is our inability to hear the other, our unwillingness to learn the language of the other, with all that that implies of unreadiness to see things from their point of view; there is our insensitivity to things that are small, our tendency to judge things by their size, our tendency to an arrogant complacency. I do not deny that these qualities characterise all nations in our fallen humanity, to some degree. But we have an uncommonly large share of them, and since the English and American peoples have been, for large parts of their history, eminently powerful and successful, their effects for better and for worse have been correspondingly magnified. For all of us the willingness to listen to the forgotten people is of life-giving importance. For us in Britain at this moment we have everything to gain from being willing to learn from a people who for many centuries have learned to live with and through external defeat.

I do not intend to write on Wales and the Welsh. But I do mean to salute and celebrate the astonishing fact that there is still a nation and a language, seven hundred years after the last of the Welsh princes was killed, four hundred years after the language was excluded from use in the affairs of law and government. I want to record the fact that against all the probabilities of economic and social pressure, there is still a vital and inventive school of writing in Welsh. In particular I want to draw attention to two facts about the

major poets who have been writing in the last forty years. Men of
great personal and literary diversity, they have nearly all been
writing from positions of strong Christian commitment. All in their
differing ways have been affirming a sacramental view of the
world, a vision of the world as full of the energies and the glories of
God. And despite the fact that, as everyone knows, it is the poetry
which gets lost when poetry is translated, I hope that something of
the wealth of what is there in modern Welsh may come through in
what I shall quote. We should, after all, most of us be rather poorly
off if we were not allowed to make contact with the psalms until we
had mastered Hebrew.

One thing must be said at the outset. The writing and reading of
poetry still has an acknowledged place in the life of Wales. The
poets are and have been since before Christian times the guardians
of the nation's memory and its sense of identity. If we are to look
for a parallel to this tradition we should turn to Russia, rather than
to England or America. When in his Nobel Prize speech
Solzhenitsyn said, 'literature becomes the living memory of a nation
. . . literature together with language preserves the national soul,' he
was saying what any Welsh writer would affirm. In going on to say
that 'the disappearance of nations would impoverish us not less than
if all men should become alike with one personality and one face.
Nations are the wealth of mankind, its generalised personalities; the
least among them has its own unique colouring and carries within
itself a unique facet of God's design,' he was speaking for all small
nations threatened with extinction. [8] The place which literature
holds in national life, whether in Russia or Wales, means that the
writer in these countries can address himself to public themes with a
directness which is rare among us today.

Of the writers to whom I am referring, three have been in prison
for conscience sake, Gwenallt for his pacifist convictions during the
first world war, Saunders Lewis for his activities as a nationalist in
the 1930s, Waldo Williams for refusing to pay taxes in support of
the Korean War in the 1950s. As well as being Christians, it goes
without saying that they are all deeply committed to their national
cause. To write in a language now spoken by little more than
500,000 people is itself an act of faith and commitment, an affirmation of the value of small, threatened, human things in the face of

the impersonal and depersonalising forces which seem to control the economic and political destinies of our time.

I have said that they all affirm a sacramental vision of the world. None does so quite as explicitly as Gwenallt in a sonnet called 'Flesh and Spirit', which begins

God has not forbidden us to love the world
And to love man and all his works,
To love them with all the naked senses,
Every shape and colour, every voice and speech;
There is a shudder in our blood when we see the trace
Of his craftsmen's fingers upon the round creation. . . .

This poem ends with the prayer that at the resurrection the spirit

Will take to itself the body, its nostrils, sight and hearing
To make sensuous the glories of God.[9]

This feeling for the bodily apprehension of the glory of God is strikingly present throughout the work of Euros Bowen, perhaps the most creative Welsh poet writing today. The method of his poetry is, as he explains, 'sacramental', and although religious themes are not often very explicitly developed in his work, religious convictions inform it through and through. This becomes particularly evident in his great and classical ode, called *Genesis*. This poem begins as a meditation on the Baptistery window in Coventry Cathedral. It has three sections, the first celebrating God's work in the seven days of creation; the second, a song to the praise of Mary in whom all creation rejoices, celebrating the work of God in the incarnation, the third hymning the activity of the Holy Spirit as the giver of life both to the believer and the Church. In this poem, as in his work more generally, the writer never lets us forget the glory of the particular object from which he begins, in this case the great window. The creative light of God shines in and through the light of every day. The two worlds are one. One of the most remarkable characteristics of the writings of Euros Bowen is the way in which the sophianic qualities which we associate with some of the best

Russian theology of our century, the quality of discerning the
wisdom and power of God at work in all things, shine out in a
work which has been shaped in the West. It is a work which grows
out of a tradition of writing which goes back to the sixth century of
our era, to a time long before the schism between the East and West
in Christendom. The poem is, of course, almost wholly unknown in
England, as is its writer, to our own great loss.

Amongst younger poets, I have already mentioned Bobi Jones. A
lecturer in the University at Aberystwyth, he is an outspoken
nationalist, an equally committed Evangelical. But when he writes
of his calling as a poet of God's court, he employs the same
language of sacramental vision.

I caught a glimpse of your court from a ridge in the Plynlimon
country;
  I saw its outskirts from a plain in Anglesey.
  I found the traces of its splendour in the breached walls of
autumn
    And the thrustfulness of spring, like one of heaven's outhouses.
    A court of justice, a king's court. My mind was open
    To wonder at its existence, and its being so compact,
    When you cried out on that part of your estate which is
to the east of Defynnog: 'You shall be a poet
    For me.' For you, Lord? For you, the Authority of life?
    'For me.' Your graces ran through the wide world;
    You stand at the table distributing your powerful wines,
    A king generous in his gifts. You leave your traces
    In a child, a wood, a church, a view,
    And in every season, Lord, you are good.
    Already in December the breeze brings forth buds
    In the lowest hour; in every countryside you manifest
    Your coming. Everything is your estate,
    And in every place there is food. Who or what
    Can give thanks sufficiently despite your atonement,
    And how shall I, O King, unlock your praise? [10]

But perhaps even more striking from the point of view of our

particular theme is a poem by a less well-known and less prolific
writer, James Nicholas. It is called 'The Bush'.

I sing to a bush that belongs
To the ancient lineage of sun and trees
In the pure earth it spreads its roots
And like the one whose hand holds it in place
It is strong, a certain strength arises
Mysteriously from the earth to give light to the tree.

I saw a fire — the green of the leaves
Was open to reach for it.
The flames rose up from the roots, creating
A great stir in the branches, and making
The boughs blossom more and more —
For there was no destroying that green growth
Rather it flourished, it grew in the fire:
The powers of life purified the bush
And before the wonder of the flowers,
The flowers of fire that knew that their growth
Over all the bush was a marvel,
I stood in thought, marvelling at it.
It was the fire which gave freshness to the earth
The fire of the liveliness of all growth.
It was the fire of visions.
It lit up the bush, it gave light to the world.

I sing to the bush, the flame of her beauty
Catches the wind and sets fire to my song:
It nurtures strength, it burns day and night,
A fire of triumph;
I sing to the bush that bonfires
The springtime of its glory
High into the air, scattering the breeze
Bringing the life of summer to the face of the earth.
I see it now lighting up my world
And the height of its vision will be praise
To God as it was in the beginning.

I climb through the fire unharmed —
Because the fire gives the growth,
And there I gather the fruit, the boughs full laden;
So pure is the season of the bush,
I will keep its harvesting against all famine
If I hold its treasure in the store of the heart.[11]

I remark on a few points in this poem. The poet declares, the
poet sees, 'I sing, . . . I sing, . . . I saw, . . . I see. . . .' It is a form of
vision and incantation which we find in some of the earliest Welsh
poetry. The senses themselves are active and at work. The whole
poem is in praise of the power of life which is at once fire and
growth. The bush is an actual bush. It is also the burning bush of the
vision of Moses. It is also the burning tree, half in leaf, half in flame,
of Welsh mythology. The powers of life springing from the earth
purify the bush, awaken the power of vision. The forces at work
within the seer, the forces at work in the world outside have one
origin and are inseparably linked. And this place and moment of
epiphany lightens the whole world, is a source of perpetual wonder,
gives rise to a harvest which can be stored in the cellars of the heart.
The interpenetration of seer and seen goes further still. The poet
climbs through the flames unharmed, like the young men in the fiery
furnace. He is caught up into that ferment of growth and creation
which our world is seen to be, when it is seen as the world in which
God is ever at work.

How is this to be done? How are the senses to be transformed?
How are the forgotten powers of natural contemplation to be
released within us? Not without discipline, not without renunciation. This is the whole work of Christian ascesis, that the perceptions may be cleansed through baptism into Christ's dying and rising again, that the senses may be sealed with the seal of the Spirit, so
that we may see with the eyes of the Dove. If we are to possess the
world and all things in it in the way in which St Francis, for instance, possessed it, we must follow the way of dispossession which
he followed.

I asked for riches.
You gave me the earth, the sea,

> the immensity
> of the broad sky. I looked at them
> and learned I must withdraw
>   to possess them. I gave my eyes
>   and my ears, and dwelt
> in a soundless darkness
>   in the shadow
>   of your regard.
>   The soul
>   grew in me, filling me
>   with its fragrance.[2]

It is only as we are finding the reality of God's action in the world within us, in the depths of the heart, that we shall be able to perceive his glory at work in the world around us. The inward and the outward visions are not alternatives but complementary, depending on each another for their growth and support. And beyond this paradox of inner and outer, there is the greater paradox of negation and affirmation. It is not for nothing that the late Byzantine vision of the divine glory radiated from the monasteries of Mount Athos, nor that in our own day one of the outstanding exponents of this mystery should have been a Cistercian monk. There is a necessary exchange between the ways of affirmation and negation. We need to find again how it is that he who loses his life will find it, that he who possesses nothing discovers he possesses all things.

Meanwhile it is clear that if the way of spirituality is to be followed anew in a time of changing consciousness, it will involve a new discovery of the place of the body and the life of the senses in our whole approach to God, our fellow-men, and the world around us. It is through the whole of human nature that God works and is present in this world of people and things. And only as our nature is being restored in God can we learn to be truly present where we are, present with all the life and love of God. 'For being with God', as Fr Benson tells us, 'is being intensely present; present where we are, as God is present where we are; present to things around us with that intense consciousness which belongs to God.' That is indeed the new consciousness which is God's own gift, and when he is present with us in that way, then we find that through the transformation of the senses the two worlds of sense and spirit, of earth and heaven have become one.

NOTES

1. Edwin Muir, *Collected Poems* (1960) pp. 198–9.
2. *The Way of a Pilgrim* (trans. R. M. French) pp. 105–6.
3. Thomas Traherne, *Poems, Centuries and Three Thanksgivings* (ed. Anne Ridler) pp. 174 and 177.
4. Mark Frank, *Works* Vol. I. (Library of Anglo-Catholic Theology) p. 100.
5. Alexander Knox, Remains, Vol I, p. 330.
6. F. J. A. Hort, *Cambridge Essays* (London 1856) pp. 292–351.
7. E. D. and F. Andrews, *Fruits of the Shaker Tree of Life* p. 74.
8. *Aleksandr Solzhenitsyn, Critical Essays and Documentary Materials*, ed. J. B. Dunlop, R. Haugh and A. Klimoff p. 567.
9. Gwenallt, *Ysgubau'r Awen* p. 85.
10. Bobi Jones, *Tyred Allan* p. 66. The translation of this and the former quotation was made by Professor H. A. Hodges.
11. *Poetry of Wales*, 1930–70 (ed. R. Gerallt Jones) pp. 335–7 (translation adapted).
12. R. S. Thomas, *Laboratories of the Spirit* p. 25.

3

Celebration

The word which stands as the title of this chapter has recently become extremely popular in certain theological circles. We hear much about the celebration of life, about man as an animal who celebrates. As often happens, a theological fashion may turn out to be the symptom of something deeper.

Certainly it would seem to be so in this case. We have here one of the signs of the breakdown of something central in our tired, strained, over-serious, over-conscious society. I propose to examine here two aspects of this breakdown, both of great importance for the rediscovery of the fullness of the Christian tradition of prayer and worship. The first is the collapse of the ethic of work, that is the conviction, often unformulated but nonetheless powerful, that you must be doing something, in the way of working at some outwardly assessable, quantifiable piece of work, if you are to justify your existence. The second is the collapse, which is just on the point of beginning, of the belief that raising the standard of living, by which in fact raising the material standard of living is always meant, is an adequate and sufficient goal for human society, and for personal life.

Both these assumptions are collapsing because they seem to have run up against a blank wall, or rather two blank walls. There is a blank wall beyond ourselves, an objective limit to the extent to which the material resources of the planet can be exploited. The question of ecology has suddenly become a burning one. If we 'raise the standard of living', that is the consumption and use of material goods, throughout the world to the level at present reached in America, it seems that we shall soon leave nothing of the planet for the use of future generations. The possibility that in the future men may discover that fullness of life is compatible with a simpler style of life, as regards material possessions, a possibility which down till ten years ago was regarded as merely romantic, and hence not to be considered, is now seriously spoken about by serious people, in other words scientific experts.

But these assumptions have also run up against another blank wall, this time an internal one. These aims, work and material production, are suddenly seen to be not in themselves worth living for. They are not necessarily either of them bad; they may in themselves be very good; but they are not sufficient. Hence this movement of protest, instinctive, unorganised, sometimes muddled and naïve, which has led young people in the United States, in Great Britain and in Western Europe to look in quite different places for fulfilment and life. These are movements which have it in common that they seek quality of life, rather than quantity, which are opposed to the cult of efficiency and acquisitiveness, which want to find time to contemplate, to celebrate, and which hope that there is in life something or someone worth contemplating, celebrating.

In general, serious people in the West, and that includes most of us over the age of twenty-five or thirty, have been so inured to the religion of work and effort, that it takes a great shock to make us realise that things can actually come to us as a gift, a grace, an unmerited surprise. Here is one of the meanings of the use of drugs, so common in some circles, as a way towards inner experience. Here too I believe is something of the significance of the gift of tongues in pentecostal groups. 'Spiritual achievement is not won only through will and effort, often it is a grace. Drugs humble the spiritual pretensions of men, effecting through the psycho-neural organism what conscious effort does not bring about.' [1]

I am not advocating an undiscriminating use of drugs. Many are very dangerous. None, even those whose use we all accept, alcohol, tobacco, medical preparations, ought to be used without discernment. But it seems to me undeniable that in some cases the use of drugs has helped people forward towards an apprehension of spiritual realities, and that in other perhaps rather rare instances, they have been used in a responsible way.[2] Michael Novak writes on this subject, 'One effect of taking drugs appears to be the capacity to perceive the world in a way which is "not American"; for the first time, some users of drugs report, they are able to look at things outside the perspective of "usefulness". It seems to be as if blinders had fallen from their eyes. Sometimes the psychological re-orientation is painful and terrifying. But often, as well, the user reports feeling liberated, seems to feel as if he were at one with the universe, and is able to notice the rich complexity and variety pre-sent even in prosaic things, like a table-top, a candle, a tree. The users of drugs report the experience not as if the world appeared suddenly chaotic and "subjective", but as if they could now see it "more objectively".

'The possibility has been raised that what seems "realistic" to the ordinary, well-educated, pragmatic, technologically orientated American is largely "subjective"; the world is perceived only insofar as it suits his purposes. The user of drugs feels liberated to perceive the world more nearly as artists, mystics and primitive people per-ceive it; the world is more alive, more personal, more resonant with unity, more terrifying, full of variety, of complexity, and of astonishing surprise. The language of *function* recedes; the language of *being* expresses the experience more accurately.' [3]

I repeat, I am not advocating the use of drugs. As this passage from Novak suggests, there are other means of discovering these things, simpler, more human, and more easily integrated with man's conscious life. But we must surely be glad, if one of the results of taking drugs can be to help some people, if only for a moment, to see the world in a less self-centred way, not to see it 'only insofar as it suits their purposes'; to be able to rejoice in its contemplation rather than its use, to see it more full of variety and surprise, and yet resonant with some underlying unity. To see the world in this way, would involve a gain in true objectivity, a breaking out of a narrow self-centredness. What is described would seem very like the vision of the world, seen in the light of God, full of the creative energies of God, which forms an important element in the growth of Christian prayer, what the Greek fathers called *physike theoria*, or natural con-templation. If, as I believe, the work of the artist, poet, painter, musician is in part to reveal these activities of God in creation, so

also it may be that the use of drugs and of the various techniques of
meditation increasingly in vogue, has a similar purpose. We are
dealing here with a vision of the world, as a world in which God is
at work, not necessarily or even probably with the direct encounter
with God himself.

As Novak points out, this way of seeing things is much more
common in pre-industrial societies, than it is in our urban world. We
go to the mountains or to the outer Hebrides to seek a world which
still seems to be transparent, to seek a silence in which a creative
word can be heard. Pre-industrial people, on the whole, seem to
have lived more closely in touch with their sub-conscious. The func-
tions of consciousness had been less developed, less strained than
they have become among us. In such cultures people knew more
easily what celebration was; something which occurs when opposites come together, when unity is achieved.

The opposites which need to come together for a celebration are
of many kinds; heart and head, feeling and thinking; conscious and
unconscious, critical intellect and intuitive intellect; experience of
time, experience of eternity; individual and group, personal and
social; myself and the world. For celebration the gulf between objective and subjective needs to be bridged. We have to go beyond
this cramping distinction, which is so obstructive to our understanding of persons, and find ourselves in a more intimate, co-
inherent relationship with others and the world around us. 'In our
culture, we are taught to make a sharp division between the self and
the world, as if the world stood opposite us "out there" whether we
noticed it or not, and as if the self were an observing consciousness,
trapped in a bag of skin. The cocktail party is our ritual symbol of
the atomic isolation of the self, each particle left free to move
whither it is attracted, each required to be mobile and to "mix".'
Here is a form of celebration certainly, but a highly individualised
one. By contrast, Novak maintains that the human person grows
through recognising a principle of openness, acknowledging the
depth of his co-inherence with the world and others. Such a view
'assumes that the subject and the range of the subject are twin poles
of one horizon, and that changes either in the subject or in his environment affect the other. The principle of openness states that the
more the subject exercises the above-mentioned operations, the more

the world, so to speak, enters into him, and he into it. The world becomes real to the subject in proportion as he experiences, understands, judges, decides; in the same proportion, the subject becomes more real (realises himself) through extending the range of the same operations, through further experiencing, understanding, judging, deciding.'[4] There is a reciprocity, an interaction, a co-inherence, between man and man, between man and nature, between man and God, in which distinction is not destroyed, but separateness is overcome, in which the opposites come together into one, and celebrate.

So far by way of introduction, we have looked at some of the considerations which help me to approach with some feeling and some understanding the Church's traditional texts on this subject, and see a little of what they mean; 'celebration' in the fully and explicitly Christian sense. Yes indeed, a coming together of opposites; creator and creation, God and man, eternity and time, life and death, holiness and sinfulness. Not that all these opposites come together in the same way; death and sinfulness cannot be equated with time, creation and man, though in our experience, they characterise all three. But in one way or another all these things come together into one in Christ, and in the gathering together of the people who are Christ's, in whom the Spirit makes possible the repentance of man before God, and opens the way to *anamnesis* and *eucharistia*, remembrance and gratitude, lifting up praise and thankfulness out of the raw material of betrayal and death. 'We celebrate the death of death, the beginning of life eternal.' [5] We give thanks in the name of him who in the night in which he was betrayed took bread.[6]

Let us take a number of examples from the great tradition, to see what is implied in this celebration.

'Wonderful, wonderful in the sight of angels, a great wonder in the eyes of faith, to see the giver of being, the generous sustainer and ruler of everything that is, in the manger in swaddling clothes and with nowhere to lay his head, and yet the bright host of glory worshipping him as a great Lord.

'O my soul, behold the place where lay the chief of kings, the author of peace, all creation moving in him, and he lying dead in the tomb; song of the lost ones and their life, chiefest wonder of the angels of heaven, they see God in flesh and worship him together in chorus, crying out "Unto him be glory."

'Thanks for ever, and a hundred thousand thanks, thanks while there is breath in me, that there is an object of worship, and a theme for a song to last for ever, in my nature, tempted like the lowest of mankind, a babe, weak, powerless, yet also the infinite, true and living God.' [7]

Around the central wonder of God in man, life in the tomb, of heaven coming down to earth, and earth lifted up to heaven, angels and men join in an ecstasy of praise, of wonder and amazement, a common expression of thanksgiving.

Next another text, by way of contrast; no less fraught with paradox and ecstasy, but moving in a more stately rhythm, the rhythm of a procession rather than a dance.

'Today the time of the feast is at hand for us; the choir of saints assembles with us, and angels join with men in keeping festival. . . . Today the Sun that never sets has risen and the world is filled with splendour by the light of the Lord. Today the moon shines upon the world with the brightness of her rays. Today the glittering stars make the inhabited earth fair with the radiance of their shining. Today the clouds drop down upon mankind the dew of righteousness from on high. Today the Uncreated of his own will accepts the laying on of hands from his own creature. Today the Prophet and Forerunner approaches the Master, but stands before him with trembling, seeing the condescension of God towards us. Today the waters of Jordan are transformed into healing by the coming of the Lord. Today the whole creation is watered by mystical streams. Today the transgressions of men are washed away by the waters of Jordan. Today Paradise has been opened to men, and the Sun of Righteousness shines down upon us. Today the bitter water, as once with Moses and the people of Israel, is changed to sweetness by the coming of the Lord. . . . Today we have been delivered from darkness and illuminated with the light of the knowledge of God. Today the blinding mist of the world is dispersed by the Epiphany of our God.' [8]

These two texts, one composed by a seventh-century Patriarch of Jerusalem, the other by an early nineteenth-century farmer's daughter in mid-Wales, testify to a common reality and a common experience. They come from the same tradition, and are the gift of one and the same Spirit. Both testify to the union of God and man, of earth and heaven, of angels and men, in and around the coming of the Christ, Jesus. There are differences of style, differences of emphasis. In Ann there is a greater concentration on the central point, the miraculous interchange of God and man in the person of the redeemer. In Sophronios there is a more expansive consideration of the cosmic consequences of God's appearing in the flesh. But it is striking that in both, this union of opposites is seen both in terms of sin and forgiveness and in terms of the restoration of all creation. Many scholars and theologians have tried to persuade us that Christianity ought to be either ethical or cosmic, that it must speak either of man's inner world or of his outer world, but that it cannot do both. These texts would suggest that precisely the reverse is true, that it is a sure sign of the wholeness of tradition when both things are held together in one. Creation and redemption, man and nature come together in the celebration of God's goodness. 'The Lord is compassionate and merciful, long suffering and of great goodness. The Lord is loving unto every man and his mercy is over all his works. All thy works praise thee, O Lord, and thy saints give thanks unto thee.' [9]

We have taken so far, to illustrate our theme of celebration, two texts from languages other than English. Let us now look at two writers from within our own English tradition. The poets and preachers of the Church of England in the seventeenth century bear a particularly rich and significant witness to this theme: Herbert, Vaughan and Traherne, Andrewes, Taylor and Mark Frank, to mention only a few representative names. Perhaps because the whole notion of liturgical celebration and of the observance of festivals was under sharp criticism from the Puritans, the Caroline divines seem to have had a particularly vivid sense of the fullness of its meaning. Perhaps too because the medieval world-view which found no difficulty in seeing a detailed correspondence between man's inner and outer world, was about to come to an end, they seem to have found special delight in considering man as a microcosm, a little world in which all the elements of the outer world are summed up.

Celebration, festival, is of many kinds, hidden and open, personal and public, silent and triumphant. I want first to cite a passage from Jeremy Taylor where he speaks of a very personal moment in the Gospel, a hidden almost silent incident. He employs to describe it all the language of the Church s liturgical tradition, so that we are forced to reflect on the way in which the Church's public celebration springs out of the inner exultation of the spirit at the coming of God, and then how that inward rejoicing is understood and interpreted in terms of what is given to all. The passage in question comes from one of the early sections of his *Life of Christ*, where he speaks of the meeting between Mary and Elizabeth, the moment called the Visitation.

'But the joys that the virgin mother had, were such as concerned all the world; and that part of them which was her peculiar, she would not conceal from persons apt to their entertainment, but go publish God's mercy towards her to another holy person, that they might join in the praises of God; as knowing that though it may be convenient to represent our personal necessities in private, yet God's gracious returns and the blessings he makes to descend upon us, are more fit, where there is no personal danger collaterally dependent, to be published in the communion of saints; that the hopes of others may receive increase, that their faith may grow up to become excellent and great, and the praises of God may be sung aloud, till the sound strike at heaven, and join with the hallelujahs which the morning stars in their orbs pay to their great Creator.

'It is not easy to imagine what a collision of joys was at this blessed meeting: two mothers of two great princes, the one the greatest that was born of women, and the other was his Lord, and these made mothers by two miracles, met together with joy and mysteriousness; where the mother of our Lord went to visit the mother of his servant, and the Holy Ghost made the meeting festival, and descended upon Elizabeth, and she prophesied. Never but in heaven was there more joy and ecstasy. The persons . . . meeting together to compare and unite their joys and their eucharist, and then made prophetical and inspired, must needs have discoursed like seraphims and the most ecstasied order of intelligences; for all the faculties of nature were turned into grace, and expressed in their way the excellent solemnity. "For it came to pass when Elizabeth heard the salutation of Mary, the babe leaped in her womb, and Elizabeth was filled with the Holy Ghost." '[10]

It would be a great mistake to think that the baroque elaboration of Taylor's style, in such a passage, was mere decoration. It has a serious purpose. He is describing the meeting of two inconspicuous women in a hill village in Palestine, no larger than the spot in mid-Wales where Ann Griffiths spent her brief life; an event outwardly beneath notice, inwardly beyond measure. The comparison of Mary and Elizabeth with the angelic orders, for instance, takes up an idea found throughout the tradition. Man, made a little lower than the angels, is in Christ crowned with a glory and honour greater than theirs, since drawn into a closer and more intimate relationship with God.[11] Therefore especially she who is the mother of the Lord, is rightly called more honourable than the cherubim and incomparably more glorious than the seraphim.[12] God in man overcomes all the impersonal powers, angelic, demonic, economic, technological which threaten to destroy human life. In its most apparently ordinary and routine aspects man's life may at every moment hide an infinite wealth of possibility, when it can open itself to the life and power of God.

But this is not perhaps the primary point which Taylor wishes to make in speaking of this meeting as one characterised by 'joy and mysteriousness'. Rather he wants to tell us something about the liturgy, the common prayer of the Church, the gathering together of God's people 'into one place'.[13] Joy and thanksgiving, he tells us, are things which grow by being shared. The united praises of men, even when two or three are gathered together, rise up before God carrying the praises of all creation with them. The liturgy is not only a meeting of man with God, it is also a meeting of man with man, a *synaxis*, a coming together into one, *epi to auto*. In this sense the meeting of Mary and Elizabeth is a beginning of Christian liturgy; two women coming together. The words which the Evangelist gives to them for this instant have remained a constant part of the Church's worship. Taylor moreover was not unaware of the Eastern Church's teaching about the work of the Holy Spirit in the Church's sacraments, and so he could write of this original moment, 'the Holy Ghost made the meeting festival'. In the power of the Spirit, man's coming together to praise God is transformed into a coming

together of man with God in the feast of the Kingdom. So too
Taylor here speaks of the incident as 'the excellent solemnity', a
term which at once recalls the words of the Latin rite, which constantly refers to the feasts of the Church, as 'joyful solemnities'.

In this very phrase, joyful or excellent solemnity, we have a junc-
tion of opposites which seems strange to our society. Are not joy
and solemnity opposed to one another? Is not a solemnity
something weighty, ponderous, ordered, ceremonious? Can it also
be something ecstatic, jubilant, spontaneous and liberating? It can,
and it must be both together if it is to answer to the fullness of man's
complex nature. Man's life cannot grow to its full human dimensions unless it is able to unite joy and sorrow, gravity and lightness,
earth and heaven in a single complex unity of love. Throughout this
passage of Taylor, there is an awareness of both, an experience of
joy and celebration which is both truth telling and truth revealing; a
mingling of what is most human with what is most divine, which is
one of the primary characteristics of all true Christian worship,
which derives from the union of God with man in Christ, itself the
heart of the message of good news. 'For all the faculties of nature
were turned into grace, and expressed in their way the excellent
solemnity.' All man's being, from its root up, is liberated into the joy
of the kingdom of God.

It is this mysterious reality which the Church seeks to express and
experience through all the changes of the liturgical year. The varying
feasts and fasts attempt to bear witness in the poverty of time to
something of the richness and the splendour of eternity. Let us look
for a moment at a feast which is at once a festival of Christ and of
his Mother, the last of the cycle of the mysteries of Christmas. Here
is Mark Frank, preaching on the feast of the Purification, sometime
in the middle of the seventeenth century.

'For this day also of his presentation, as well as those of his birth,
circumcision and manifestation – Candlemas day as well as
Christmas day, New Year's day or Epiphany, is a day of blessing; a
day of God's blessing us and our blessing him again; of Christ's being presented for us, and our presenting to him again; of his
presenting in the temple, and our presenting ourselves in the Church,
to bless God and him for his presentation, his presentation-day and
our Candlemas, our little lights, our petty lights; our souls reflecting

back to this great light that was this day presented in the temple and
then darted down upon us.' [14]

The very multiplicity of the festivals of God's manifestation in
the flesh reveals something of the riches of God's mercy. The divine
energies are manifold, not to be expressed in a single image, in a
single festival. The divine nature, and mankind made in its image, is
as richly diverse as it is profoundly one. Hence the Church's
festivals serve to draw together the multitude of men in all their
diversity. 'The shepherds blessed God in the morn of his nativity;
the wise men upon Epiphany; Simeon and Anna today. All conditions before, all sexes today; ignorant shepherds and learned clerks,
poor countrymen and great princes, no condition out before, both
sexes in today. Sinners both of Jew and Gentile, men that most
stood in need of a saviour before; just and righteous souls today;
that we might know that there is none so good but stand in need of
him one day or another – that will want a saviour, if not at
Christmas, yet at Candlemas; if not among sinners, yet among the
righteous, first or last. Mary the blessed, Joseph the just, Simeon the
devout, Anna the religious, all in today, secular and religious, of all
sexes and orders; all come in today, as at the end of Christmas; like
the chorus to the angels' choir, to bear a part in the angels' anthem,
to make up a full choir of voices to glorify God for this great present, which brings peace to earth and good-will towards men.' [15]

Therefore, concludes the preacher, at this end of Christmas, let all
come together into one. Inward and outward rejoice with one accord. Let man become the spokesman of the whole creation. Let all
things enter into the dance of praise. 'Call to all the creatures to bear
you company – everything to rejoice with you. Tell your happiness
to the woods and mountains, in your solitary retirements; tell it to
the towns and villages. Speak of it in all companies; tell it to the
young men and maids, old men and children, all sexes and ages,
what God has done for your souls. Tell it to the summer and winter,
both in your prosperity and adversity; let nothing make you forget
your thanks. Tell it to the frost and fire, in your coldnesses and in
your fervencies and zeals; to the earth and to the waters, in your
dryness of soul and in the sorrows of your hearts; praise him in all
conditions . . . entreat them all, all states and orders, all conditions
and things to bring in each their blessing, to make up one great and

worthy blessing for this day's blessing, to rejoice and sing, exult and triumph with you for this happy armful of eternal blessings this day bestowed upon you.' [16]

With such a wealth of wisdom and experience at the heart of our common Christian tradition, it seems strange that we should have to turn aside to drugs, or to other faiths to find again in our own time the meaning of celebration. Has our failure been due, in part, to the way in which we have neglected the life of the senses, have sought to celebrate God in an immaterial way, not seeing that he is to be praised in and through his whole creation, and that all the faculties of our nature are to be turned into grace? The very circumstances of our time which force upon us a new awareness of the *oikoumene*, the whole inhabited earth, drive us back to find again the treasures hidden within our common tradition; that tradition, which in its fullness and balance is called Orthodoxy, which, though it has its home in the Christian East, has not by God's grace wholly abandoned us in the West. There we find again that sober drunkenness, that waking ectasy of which the Fathers speak. There indeed we find that we may be liberated in our perceptions so that we may see this world not only insofar as it suits our purposes, but as it is in itself, when it is known as the work of a merciful creator, 'more alive, more personal, more resonant with unity, more terrifying, full of variety, of complexity and of astonishing surprise'. As the language of function and utility recedes, so the language of being and rejoicing comes to the fore. We learn again to see the world in God, and are enabled to celebrate the goodness and glory of him from whom and to whom all things proceed.

NOTES

1. In *The Religious Situation: 1968*, ed. Donald R. Cutler (Beacon Press, Boston), the article by Michael Novak, 'The New Relativism in American Theology' p. 206.

2. See for instance pp. 87–92 in *Travelling In* by Monica Furlong (London 1971).

3. op. cit. pp. 206–7, italics original.

4. ibid. pp. 213–14.

5. From the Easter Canon of St John of Damascus.

6. The constructive significance of 'taking bread' in the hour of betrayal is too little considered, in thought about the institution narrative.

7. For the full text of this hymn see the article by Saunders Lewis, 'Ann Griffiths; A literary survey' in *Homage to Ann Griffiths* (Church in Wales Publications 1976).

8. Mother Mary and Father Kallistos Ware, *The Festal Menaion* (London 1969) pp. 354–5.

9. Psalm 145:8–10.

10. Jeremy Taylor, *The Whole Works etc.*, Edition of 1835, Vol I pp. 31–2.

11. Psalm 8:4–5.

12. cf. The Byzantine hymn, 'More honourable than the cherubim . . .'

13. This phrase, in the Greek *epi to auto*, occurs more than once in the Book of the Acts to describe the unanimity of the Christian gathering. See e.g. Acts 2:2 and also I Cor. 11:20.

14. Mark Frank, *Sermons*, Vol. I, L.A.C.T. p. 340 from the First Sermon on the Purification.

15. ibid. p. 341.

16. ibid. p. 372, from the latter part of the Second Sermon for this feast.

II

THE RESTORATION OF MAN

4

The Communion of Saints

At the heart of the Christian way there is a single life and a single death, which though it is situated in space and in time, is, it is asserted, not limited by these things in the way in which our lives usually are. In a particular place and at a particular moment in history something new occurred, which had about it all the newness of the creation itself. The barriers of death were broken down, so that all times and all places, the ages which came before as well as the ages which follow after, are affected by this radically new and creative act. God is in man, and man is taken into God. The things of God become the things of man, and what is most distinctively divine becomes most distinctively human. Man at last realises in himself that for which he was made, that for which he has always longed. He becomes truly man in coming to share fully in the very life and nature of God.

This is the faith which lies behind the words 'the communion of saints', a phrase which originally implied a sharing in holy things (the things of God) by holy persons (the people of God). Holiness, which is the very characteristic of God, is a self-communicating principle, it desires to share itself. And through the passage from life through death to life in God which, it is affirmed, took place in the exodus of Jesus of Nazareth, God himself, the Holy Spirit, the giver of all holiness has come to communicate himself in a new way, to dwell in the midst of human life. Men find that in many surprising ways they are joined to one another and to God in this transcendent gift. The forces which bind down and destroy the life of man are overcome in the presence of one who is God not of the dead but of the living; for all live to him.

This triumph over death through death is explicitly made ours in the Church's sacraments, which are all of them re-enactments of that original event, Christ's Passover and the coming of the Spirit. But what is given in the sacraments in symbolic act, is worked out day by day in the very texture of Christian living and dying, so that the events which took place in Jerusalem two thousand years ago are not imprisoned in the past but become living and active in the present. These are the things which unite all the Christian centuries, and which, despite all the divisions men have made, unite all the Christian traditions in a single communion of life.

Sometimes this becomes particularly evident at the very moment when the believer himself approaches the threshhold of death, when his death is finally to be included in his master's death. Here is a Nestorian Bishop in what is now Iraq, in the ninth century, about to die, 'And our holy father Mar Abraham the Catholicos told me, saying, "While many of us were gathered together about him at the hour of his departure, he sat and spake with us concerning his separation from us. And he commanded us to say the response of Baptism, 'The doors of the spiritual marriage chamber are opened for the absolution of men,' while he sat with his hands laid upon his knees. And when we had come to the passage, 'Enter in then ye that are called to the joy which has been prepared for you,' he opened his mouth three times to join in the singing, and his soul departed from his body with the joy which was prepared for him. And marvelling, we understood that he actually saw and beheld with the hidden eye of his mind the happiness which had been prepared for him, and that it was because of this he had asked us to sing the baptismal response." ' The words of the hymn which they were singing were as follows:

Open unto me the gates of righteousness —
the gates of heaven are opened.
The gates of the spiritual marriage chamber of the Bridegroom
are opened for the forgiveness of the sins of men,
and through the gift of the Spirit from on high,
mercy and peace are now vouchsafed to all mankind.

Enter in therefore, O ye who are called –
enter into the joy which is prepared for you,
and with pure and sanctified hearts and true faith,
give thanks to Christ our Saviour.

. . . .

O thou true Door open to the lost
and call us to enter thy treasury on high. [1]

'In my end is my beginning.' The initial conformity of his life to the
life and death and resurrection of Christ conferred in baptism
through the coming of the Spirit (in whom we die with him that we
may be raised with him), worked out through all the painful yet
joyful years of faith and prayer, of obedience and love in action,
flowers at the final moment, so that those who are standing by can
see in the face of the one they had been thinking to console, the ultimate and only consolation and fulfilment of all the longings of the
heart of man.

Here is a seventeenth-century Englishman, a man who had considerable contact with the intellectual and political life of his time,
the years before the Civil War, similarly surrounded at the moment
of his death by his friends and family, that family which he had
welded into an unforgettable community at Little Gidding. 'Towards evening he called the family and other friends together . . . and
asked them to say the prayers for a dying man. He seemed to fall
into a peaceful sleep for a time, but they remained with him in the
room. Suddenly he raised himself up in bed. His voice came clear
and strong and, stretching out his arms, he looked upward and
around him with a light of great happiness in his eyes. "Oh what a
blessed change is here," he cried. "What do I see . . . I have been at
a great feast. O magnify the Lord with me." One of his nieces spoke
to him. "At a feast, dear father?" "Aye," he answered, "at a great
feast, the great King's feast." They stood in awe waiting for him to
continue. But he sank back quietly on his bed and closed his eyes . . .
His lips parted and he gave a long gasp. In that moment they saw
that his soul was sped. At the same instant the clock struck one – it
was the hour at which for years past he had always risen for his
morning devotions.' [2] So to the very end the rhythms of bodily life,
of sleeping and waking, were maintained. Only now, he rose up

finally and definitively into that presence and that joy, which day by day he had risen up, who knows with how much effort, to find. For the thing above all which unites those two men across the centuries is that like Bishop Elijah, Nicholas Ferrar was a man of constant and unceasing prayer. Both, through all the differences of their times, had given a large part of their life, waking and sleeping, to the things which belong to eternity, standing on the threshhold of that marriage feast into whose fullness they were now being called to enter.

To say such things as these, at least to say them with any seriousness, is to make large affirmations about the nature of human life, which the greater part of the daily experience of most of us hardly seems to corroborate. It is to say that man's life is lived on the verge of an unbelievable fulfilment, and that even here and now through all the fragmentation, the waste, the tragedy of our existence that fulfilment is made known. Here and now we are being drawn into it. Even here and now there is something unspeakably wonderful about human life when it is received as God's gift and lived in His presence. We share our life 'with angels and archangels and all the company of heaven'. The world of time and the world of eternity are nearer to each other than we usually think. There is a good deal of coming and going between them.

Moreover, although (in the past at least) Christians of almost every persuasion have taken this faith in the communion of saints seriously, and have found much joy in it — one might think of the great Puritan writer of the seventeenth century, Richard Baxter, both in his prose and in his verse — it is true that there has been a good deal of controversy about how it is to be understood, and how we are to express it. Should we pray for the departed? Should we ask them directly to pray for us? How far, in this life, can this interchange of divine and human gifts already be realised? Can we indeed see the glory of God in the very faces of his saints? There are genuine questions here. Even if they do not press upon us, as they did on people in the past, they deserve our attention, for they can still divide Christians from one another in painful ways, and can still prevent us from entering into the fullness of our inheritance.

The questions which the reformers of the sixteenth century put might be formulated thus. Is there not a great danger that the cult of the saints could become a substitute for the worship of God in Christ? Has it not in fact at times become such a substitute, a distraction from the one thing necessary, on which the New Testament is so clear and so insistent, that we should come to know Christ, and in the power of the Spirit, learn to approach God as our Father through him? What need have we for any other mediators than him? What profit is there in asking for the prayers of those departed this life, what warrant in Scripture for our praying for them?

First let us say, with the great Russian theologian of the nineteenth century, Alexei Khomiakov, that the whole question is liable to be misconceived if it is posed in terms of 'necessity' and 'profit'. Prayer is never a matter of profit and necessity, but of freedom and love. We pray for the departed because we love them in the love which comes from God, and believing them to be nearer God than we are, we are sure that they pray for us more strongly within that same love. In prayer, by God's gift, man rises up into the freedom of God and becomes a fellow-worker with God. For Khomiakov, to ask the departed to pray for us, and ourselves to pray for them is a natural expression of our solidarity with them in the redemptive love of God in Christ. It is a gift of the Holy Spirit, an aspect of that communion and fellowship which he creates.

But we need not go as far as Russia to receive such an assurance. Within our own tradition we can find authorities enough. Here is William Forbes, first Bishop of Edinburgh, who died in 1634, a contemporary of Nicholas Ferrar, speaking on this very question. 'The Fathers certainly were led ... by the testimonies and examples of Scripture to conclude that it is evident that the prayers which just men offer for others are of great avail with God. They were moreover certainly persuaded that the righteous at their death do not cease to be, but joined to Christ, lead a blessed life, and that they pray for us now more ardently than before, inasmuch as they are endued with greater love than formerly, and, as Cyprian says, "are secure in their own immortality and anxious for our safety". The Fathers, therefore, I say, desired very greatly that during their pilgrimage in this life they might be aided by the prayers of those who were reigning in heaven, (a thing which no one will say is unlawful), and even asked for it, so far namely as the saints have knowledge of our condition. For although it be altogether uncertain whether they have an *idiopatheia* (to use the expression of some Protestants), that is, a particular acquaintance with our necessities and distresses, yet, who in his senses would deny them a *sumpatheia*, or general knowledge, derived from the word of God and their own experience? And the Fathers declared this their wish and desire, by calling upon them, either all in general, or even some particular individuals by name, both in their public and their private prayers, as being present with them in spirit and in soul. Not that they made them chief or propitiatory mediators with God, but that by their prayers which they believed to be of great avail with God, joined to their own prayers, they might more readily obtain their desires from God the Father, through Jesus Christ, the only mediator and propitiator.'[3]

Yes, it is true that we could make a cult of the saints which obscured the unique glory of the Lord Christ. It may well be that at some times and places Christians have done so. But it is not a great threat to us in the last quarter of the twentieth century. Nor is it likely to become so, so long as we remember that it is the light of the one Lord Christ which shines out in all the infinite variety of their lives and which draws us to them. What we have done, and are much more likely to do, is to empty heaven of its citizens, leaving a Lord remote and isolated, with whom we find it hard to come into contact. The Gospel narratives themselves take on a new closeness and a new relevance, when we read them in the light which comes from those who have lived them most intensely. Through the lives of the saints the life of their one Lord and Master becomes real for us in new ways. Furthermore, by our failure to help people to pray with and for their own friends and family who have died, we have denied one of the deepest instincts of the human heart, and driven people into various forms of spiritualism. Concern for the departed can take genuinely unbalanced and unhealthy forms, when we attempt to come into contact with them for our own ends and on our own terms. To do so almost inevitably trivialises the mystery of death, as anyone who has had to read spiritualist literature can testify. This is a danger unexpectedly present in our own day. The failure of the Church to make it plain that it is only in God that we can rightly have fellowship with the departed, has much to do with this situation.

For the fact that people wish to pray for those who have died does not make the practice wrong, even though it may be difficult to find in the New Testament an explicit command for it. There is certainly nothing there which would make it forbidden. Another Anglican writer of the seventeenth century, Herbert Thorndike, Prebendary of Westminster in the years immediately following the Commonwealth, indeed puts the matter more positively. Read in the light of constant Christian practice, he maintains it is an integral part of our heritage of faith. 'There is the same ground to believe the communion of saints in the prayers which those that depart in the highest favour with God make for us; in the prayers which we make for those that depart in the lowest degree of favour with God, that there is for the common Christianity; namely the Scripture interpreted by the perpetual practice of God's Church. Therefore there is ground enough for the faith of all Christians, that those prayers are accepted which desire God to hear the saints for us, to send the deceased in Christ rest and peace and light and refreshment, and a good trial at the day of judgment and accomplishment of happiness after the same.' [4]

But who are these saints with whom we are said to be in communion? Not, clearly, only those who are called 'Saints', who by one means or another have been publicly recognised and commemorated by the Church as people who have reflected the character of God in some particularly shining way. Rather it must include all those who belong to God, to the God who is not a God of the dead but of the living, all those who are in Christ, and are united with us in the power of the Holy Spirit. Whether, or in what way, one can live and die in Christ without having heard the preaching of the Gospel or been baptised into the Church is not a question to be treated here. But if we seriously believe that the redemptive power of Christ's death and resurrection works backwards in time as well as forwards, we shall, I believe, have to affirm that it is possible. The Orthodox icon of the resurrection shows the victorious Christ raising up our first parents Adam and Eve, the representatives of all humanity. 'As in Adam all die, even so in Christ shall all be made alive.' We must not narrow the scope of God's activity and God's love. But for our purpose here it is enough to say that all the departed in Christ pray for us and we pray for all of them. The distinction which Thorndike makes between those who die in the highest favour with God, whose prayers we naturally seek, and those who die in the lowest favour with God, for whom we are most strongly drawn to pray, though useful, is not rigid or exclusive. All are united with all. Those whom the Churches officially recognise as 'Saints' (for the Orthodox Church has its ways of canonisation, as well as the Roman Catholic; and the Anglican Communion is not wholly deprived of ways of making public recognition of God's servants) are simply those in whom the Christian people recognise some outstanding manifestation of the one life in Christ which is common to all. It is because all are called to be saints, that the Church is able to recognise in some the outstanding generosity of response to a call which all share.

And what a glory of generosity is revealed in the lives and faces of the Saints! In them the true dimensions of our common humanity begin to become apparent. 'The human heart can go to the lengths of God.' There is in man a capacity for suffering and for joy, for love and for knowledge which too often we hardly suspect. Our wounded and deeply pessimistic age has too small a regard for the nature and dignity of man. The concentration camps of so many nations, the bombs dropped on Dresden and Hiroshima, the methods of warfare employed on both sides in Vietnam, tell us what we think about man. We look at the faces round about us in the tube, we look at the face before us in the mirror, and ask What is man? We turn on the radio and the news bulletins tell us every day that he is simply a being who fights for higher wages. The advertisements assure us that his happiness consists in consuming a great many expensive objects. We go into the Tate and look at the pictures of Francis Bacon, we read works of great imagination and we find that man is a 'useless passion', or rather a random bundle of useless and destructive passions without meaning or coherence.

And then we find in the darkest places that the light has shone. In the concentration camps a Mother Maria has been present, bringing even there a certain calm, a gleam of joy until the moment when she took the place of another in the line which led to the gas chambers. We find a Secretary-General of the United Nations, at the centre of the world's largest international bureaucracy, leading a life of intense communion with God, and able to say even there, 'For all that has been, Thanks. To all that shall be, Yes.' We open the pages of Solzhenitsyn and are reminded again that in apparently hopeless situations there is a stubborn integrity, a depth of humanness which renews our hope, and makes us proud to be a human being. An eminent Romanian intellectual said to me, 'After reading Solzhenitsyn I felt for the first time that the Russians are our brothers; that we share a common humanity.' 'The just shall live by faith.' Yes, and the world will live by that faith of the Saints, those who have not despaired, who in the darkness have seen light, and have therefore been able to bring light and hope to a whole people.

These are not only men and women of our own day. Here time and space no longer divide. A young monk on Mount Athos has recently written, 'I am reading St Isaac the Syrian. I feel for the first time that there is a voice which resonates in the very depths of my being. Although he is so far removed from me in space and time, he has come right into my room, spoken to me, sat down beside me. For the first time I feel a kind of pride in our human nature, an amazement before it . . . He belongs to our common humanity. I rejoice at this. Being of the same nature as myself, he can transfuse the life-giving blood of this freedom into me. He reveals to me man in his true nature.' And this experience is not one which is foreign to us. How often on reading a Kierkegaard for instance, or on reading the life of some man or woman of God, we have felt the words coming off the page and hitting us, have felt the writer with us in the room. Merton became a friend for thousands of people who had never met him in the flesh. In this way, St Francis has been constantly interfering in the affairs of the Church of England in the last hundred years or so, sending off respectable clergymen to live in the slums, inciting sensible laymen with good prospects, to become vagrant with the vagrants, to rediscover the solitary life of prayer and silence, to begin again to show us something of the true glory of man.

Another thing has begun to happen in our days which is not unconnected with all this. The holy places have begun to come to life. Who but Dr Johnson in the eighteenth century would have thought that Iona would have become such a powerful place again? Even he would have been silenced by the fact that St Columba should become such a presence for so many eminent Presbyterians. Who could have foreseen the revival of pilgrimage to Lindisfarne and Glastonbury, or still more surprisingly, to Walsingham? What is it which draws people to such places? It is the presence of the saints and the prayers of the saints.

> For wherever a saint has dwelt, wherever a martyr has given his blood for the blood of Christ,
> There is holy ground, and the sanctity shall not depart from it,
> Though armies trample over it, though sightseers come with guide-books looking over it . . .[5]

The instinct to go to places where people have lived, (think of Stratford-upon-Avon) is not a wholly vain one. It is one thing to know that George Herbert gave up a promising career in Cambridge and London in order to bury himself in an insignificant country parish. It is another to kneel before the altar in the tiny church at Bemerton. It is one thing to know that at a time of great danger during the war George Bell and Dietrich Bonhoeffer met in Sweden, transcending all the conflict in a relationship established in Christ. It is another thing to sit in the quiet house in Sigtuna where the meeting actually took place. There are other places in England too, though they are little enough noticed, which are places where prayer has taken root: Kingscliffe, for many years the home of William Law; Hursley where Keble ministered for thirty years and himself built the church. Our own lives and the life of our nation are not so full of places of epiphany that we can afford to neglect them. They are part of our eucharist and our *anamnesis*, our recalling of the things that God has done, and our thanksgiving for them. For the lives of God's friends often seem in a strange way to gather up and fulfil the aspirations of a whole people. What is true and characteristic of a nation or a country in them is not lost, but transfigured.

For the communion of saints is never an abstract or ethereal thing, a piece of superfluous doctrine. It is rooted in this earth, in places where people have lived and loved, and seen the glory of God shining out in the common light of every day. But those who have been constantly with God in prayer have even in this life become somewhat freer of time and space than most of us are. In prayer we come more intimately into touch with those unconscious levels of our being which seem to be less tied to the time sequence than our consciousness is. Beyond them we begin to enter into the deep places of the Spirit. Perhaps this is why, even after centuries of neglect, holy places are still found to be full of a timeless presence.

> If you came this way
> Taking any route, starting from anywhere,
> At any time or at any season,
> It would always be the same: you would have to put off
> Sense and notion. You are not here to verify,
> Instruct yourself, or inform curiosity
> Or carry report. You are here to kneel
> Where prayer has been valid. And prayer is more
> Than an order of words, the conscious occupation
> Of the praying mind, or the sound of the voice praying.
> And what the dead had no speech for, when living,
> They can tell you being dead: the communication
> Of the dead is tongued with fire beyond the language of the
> living,[6]

We have come back to Little Gidding, one of the places from which we started. It is not surprising that we should find in T. S. Eliot such a sure guide to an understanding of the communion of saints. For he joined to the intuition of faith, a massive sense of the meaning of tradition, conceived not as the preservation of certain relics from the past, but as the presence with us now of powers of life and understanding without whom we should indeed be orphans. What he saw primarily in terms of literature, is true in a deeper and more universal sense of the tradition of the Church. Without it we should indeed be comfortless. But he who is Lord alike of life and death has promised that he will not leave us bereft. 'In the gift of the Spirit from on high, mercy and peace are now vouchsafed to all mankind': all men find themselves one family in God our Father.

NOTES

1. *The Book of Governors: The Historia Monastica of Thomas Bishop of Marga. A.D. 840*, ed. E. A. Wallis Budge, Vol. II pp. 518–19.

2. A. L. Maycock, *Nicholas Ferrar of Little Gidding* (1963) pp. 299–300.
3. William Forbes, *Works*, Vol. II, L.A.C.T. pp. 229–31. (It is difficult to know why such a man should be called an *Anglican*. Scottish by birth and upbringing, receiving all his education in Scotland, or on the continent of Europe, he is one of those witnesses who remind us that there is nothing limitingly English about that form of Christian tradition which is commonly called Anglican.)
4. Herbert Thorndike, *Works*, Vol. V, L.A.C.T. p. 249.
5. T. S. Eliot, *Murder in the Cathedral*.
6. T. S. Eliot, *Little Gidding*.

Wholeness and Transfiguration

In the past century Anglicans have sometimes thought of the recovery of the religious life as the supreme vindication of the catholicity of the Church to which they belong, and surely not without justification. But perhaps more deeply we can think of it as an implicit affirmation of the unity of the Church across the barriers which at present divide us from one another. It is an affirmation that the heritage of the first centuries is still a vital reality in the Church today, that St Anthony and St Pachomius, St Benedict and St Basil, St David and St Columba are living powers within our own Church, as they are within the Church of Rome or the Church of Eastern Orthodoxy. An affirmation that this unity is particularly realised and declared when the Churches live from the power of the Spirit, in complete dependence on Jesus Christ our Lord; when our faith in the holiness of the Church, its participation in the divine life, ceases to be a formula which we repeat and becomes an experienced reality of daily life.

So it is that the founders of our communities would have been, I believe, in deep accord with the Russian Metropolitan in Paris between the two wars, Metropolitan Eulogy, when he declared, 'Men like St Seraphim, St Francis of Assisi and many others have in their lives accomplished the union of the Churches. Are they not citizens of the same holy and universal Church? At the level of their spiritual life they have gone beyond the walls which divide us, but which, in the fine expression of Metropolitan Platon of Kiev, do not reach up to heaven.'[1] Not only in the lives of the great saints, though there

pre-eminently, but wherever the life of prayer is being truly and
authentically lived, there the unity of the Church is being made
known, through the healing action of the Holy Spirit. There too is
revealed another kind of unity, that which exists between different
expressions of the religious or monastic ideal, a unity which makes
that diversity a source of enrichment, not of narrowness or division.
One of the lesser-known figures of the twelfth-century monastic
revival in France affirms this clearly:

> In my Father's house there are many mansions, and there are
> many ways which lead to it. These various ways have been com-
> mended in writing by divers of the Fathers, and they are called
> the Rules of St Basil, St Augustine and St Benedict. These are
> not the sources of the religious life, but only its offshoots, they are
> not the root but the leaves. The Rule from which all others
> derive, like streams flowing from a single source, is the Holy
> Gospel.[2]

What I want to do in this essay is to examine this assertion of unity a little more closely in relation to precisely the two saints mentioned by Metropolitan Eulogy, St Francis and St Seraphim. I
believe that we shall find that the unity of which they tell us is not
only an ecclesiastical unity in the narrow sense of that word. Rather
it is a unity, an integration of each one of us within himself, and also
a unity, an integration of each one of us with all our fellow men, and
indeed with all creation. It is only when man begins to rediscover
himself as both microcosm, the one in whom the world is summed
up, and mediator, the one through whom the world is offered to
God, that the divisions of the Churches will begin to be healed. For
only in such a perspective are the true dimensions of human unity
revealed, and its Godward direction made plain. The unity for
which our Lord prays is based in God himself; it is a unity which is
for all men and not against them, for all creation and not against it,
since God himself is Father, Redeemer, and Sanctifier of all.

In coming to understand the nature of this work of unification,
this restoration of wholeness, I believe we have much to learn from
those, many of them outside the Churches, who in our own century
have studied man's nature at depth from the view-point of psychol-

ogy. They help the theologian to give flesh and blood to concepts and traditions which are in danger of remaining dis-incarnate, too exalted to be rooted in man's creatureliness. Thomas Merton, for instance, in his essay on 'Final Integration', in *Contemplation in a World of Action*, as we have seen makes extensive use of the work of the Persian psychiatrist, Reza Arasted. He re-opens for us an understanding of what it means to find that the human person, when approaching the fullness of life and being, becomes catholic, universal. The fully integrated man 'is in a certain sense "cosmic", and "universal man".' He has attained a deeper, fuller identity than that of his limited ego-self which is only a fragment of his being. He is in a certain sense identified with everybody, or in the familiar language of the New Testament . . . he is "all things to all men".' [3] He is freed from the limitations of a particular cultural tradition, though not uprooted from it. He no longer has to affirm his identity against others. He can be *for* every one.

A very similar affirmation is to be found in a book written by a French Franciscan in exposition of St Francis's great poem, 'The Canticle of the Creatures'. In this remarkable work, Fr Eloi Leclerc contends, in a way which reveals a clear influence of Jungian ideas, St Francis's celebration of the creatures, sun and moon, earth and air, fire and water, life and death, is not only an act of acknowledgement of the created world around him, but also of the unconscious depths within, of the great archetypal powers which lie within him. In this way the author reactivates the ancient idea of man as a microcosm, and of a correspondence betwen man's inner world and the outer world in which he is placed. 'In opening himself to the world, in taking his place among the creatures, in becoming profoundly aware of them as "brothers" and "sisters", Francis also opened himself to that obscure part of himself which is rooted in nature; unconsciously he was fraternising with his own depths.' [4]

Thus reconciled with his own living powers, with his whole effective nature . . . man is born into a new personality, as large as the universe, open to the whole of being, welcoming to the mystery of the Other, in all its otherness. As brother of the sun and of all creation, Francis can go forward . . . free from all defensive reactions, all turning in on himself. In a violent world, bristling with castles, divided up by fortifications, as was that of the Middle Ages, his universe was without walls and fortresses. He was without frontiers.[5]

Here indeed is a restatement of that ancient vision of the inter-penetration of man and the universe which is wonderfully expressed in the writings of the Fathers. 'Be on peaceful terms with thy soul; then heaven and earth will be on peaceful terms with thee. Be zealous to enter the treasury within; then thou wilt see that which is in heaven. For the former and the latter are one, and entering thou wilt see both. The ladder into the Kingdom is hidden within thy soul. Dive into thyself, freed from sin; there thou wilt find steps along which thou canst ascend.'[6] In England this same vision found a late but eloquent expression in the seventeenth century in the writings of Thomas Traherne.

You will never enjoy the world aright, till the sea itself floweth in your veins, till you are clothed with the heavens and crowned with the stars ... till your spirit filleth the whole world, and the stars are your jewels, till you are familiar with the way of God in all ages as with your walk and table ... till you delight in God for being good to all: you never enjoy the world.[7]

Here is a cosmic and personal vision of life and unity, a vision which answers in a curious way to one of the acutest problems of our own time, the problem of the pollution and destruction of the environment. Very rapidly men are becoming aware that the lack of balance in their relationship with the material world around them arises from a lack of balance within themselves. The problem of pollution cannot be separated from the problem of inner alienation and disharmony, any more than it can be separated from the problem of harmony between men, the questions of social justice. All three dimensions of the questions – personal, social, cosmic – belong together, and though they may properly be distinguished they cannot be separated one from another.

Leclerc makes this point very forcefully when he comes to comment on the verse in the Canticle in praise of those who pardon and forgive. Though it is true that this verse was added after the composition of the main part of the song, he argues that it is by no means an accidental or merely occasional addition. Rather it reveals and completes the meaning of the whole. There is a profound link between 'the verses of cosmic praise, and the verse given over to pardon and peace'.[8] 'The Canticle is truly seen as the song of the man who is fully reconciled and at peace, in his relations with others, with himself.' It is to be understood not as a nostalgic longing for a lost paradise but as 'a vision of the world, dominated by the primacy of conciliation over discord, of unity over division . . . and this unity and this fulness are not to be sought by turning back to a primitive state of sleep, but through a deeper presence to oneself and to others.'[9] We cannot make a separation between our attitude towards people and our attitude towards things. 'The will towards reconciliation which inspires and characterizes all Francis' human relations goes closely together with his attitude of brotherliness, of a very deep, felt communion with the most humble elements of the cosmos.'[10] We can not, whatever we may commonly think, 'combine an attitude of respect, welcome, and sympathy towards our fellow human beings, with an attitude of aggression, conquest and domination towards the whole of the rest of nature.'[11]

Thus Francis lived at one with all creation. His relations with the animals are perhaps the most widely remembered of all his characteristics, though not everyone remembers that he preached to fish as well as to birds, and would remove worms from the path so that they should not be trodden on. And here at once is one of the traits he shares in common with St Seraphim. In his years in the forest, St Seraphim lived very close to the animals, and had a particular friendship for the bears. Contrary to what is often said today, St Francis is not exceptional in his attitude towards the natural world, the animal kingdom. Rather, one might say, he gives an outstanding example of something which is seen in all the saints, but particularly in the saints of the Orthodox East. For in Orthodoxy this awareness of man's cosmic vocation has never been lost to sight, has never ceased to be an integral part of the vision of man's redemption.

As Vladimir Lossky puts it, in *The Mystical Theology of the Eastern Church*, resuming the teaching of St Maximus the Confessor, 'Man is not a being isolated from the rest of creation; by his very nature he is bound up with the whole of the universe . . . In his way

to union with God, man in no way leaves creatures aside, but
gathers together in his love the whole cosmos disordered by sin, that
it may at last be transfigured by grace.' [12] To illustrate this point he
quotes a remarkable passage from St Isaac the Syrian, a spiritual
writer still highly commended in Orthodox monastic circles:

> What is a charitable heart? It is a heart which is burning with
> love for the whole creation, for men, for the birds, for the beasts,
> for the demons — for all creatures. He who has such a heart can-
> not see or call to mind a creature without his eyes being filled
> with tears by reason of the immense compassion which seizes his
> heart; a heart which is softened and can no longer bear to see or
> learn from others of any suffering, even the smallest pain, being
> inflicted upon a creature. That is why such a man never ceases to
> pray also for the animals, for the enemies of truth, and for those
> who do him evil, that they may be preserved and purified. He
> will pray even for the reptiles, moved by the infinite pity which
> reigns in the hearts of those who are becoming united with
> God.[13]

There is no reason to suppose that St Francis and his first disciples were acquainted with the writings of St Isaac. But the description of the loving heart applies at once to the man of Assisi, whose
companions report, 'We who were with him have seen him take inward and outward delight in almost every creature, and when he
handled or looked at them his spirit seemed to be in heaven rather
than on earth.'[14] Nor is it likely that any but the most indirect influence of the teaching of Maximus the Confessor had reached thir-
teenth-century Italy. But we can hear clearly the theme of what the
Greek fathers called *physike theoria*, the contemplation of God in his
creation, in this passage from the first of Francis's biographers:

> He rejoiced in all the works of the hands of the Lord and saw
> behind all things pleasant to behold their life-giving reason and
> cause. In beautiful things he saw Beauty itself, all things were to
> him good. 'He Who made us is the best,' they cried out to him.
> Through his footprints impressed upon all things he followed the
> Beloved everywhere; he made for himself from all things a ladder

by which to come even to his throne. He embraced all things
with a rapture of unheard of devotion, speaking to them of the
Lord and admonishing them to praise him. . . . He forbade the
brothers to cut down the whole tree when they cut wood, so that
it might have hope of sprouting again. He commanded the gar-
dener to leave the border around the garden undug, so that in
their proper times the greenness of the grass and the beauty of the
flowers might announce the beauty of the Father of all things. He
commanded that a little place be set aside in the garden for sweet-
smelling and flowering plants, so that they would bring those
who looked upon them to the memory of the Eternal Sweetness.
He removed from the road little worms, lest they be crushed under foot; and he ordered that honey and the best wines be set out
for the bees, lest they perish from want in the cold of winter. He
called all animals by the name 'brother', though among all kinds
of animals he preferred the gentle. Who could possibly narrate
everything? For that original goodness that will one day be all
things and in all was already shown forth in this saint as all
things in all.[15]

The terms of the final sentence in this passage need particularly to
be noted. That original goodness, that is to say, the creative power
of God who 'saw all that he had made and behold, it was very
good', will one day, in the end of all things, be all in all, when
things are gathered together in that final fulfilment which the
Gospel figures for us in the feast of the Kingdom. Even now that
goodness which is declared in him who is the first and the last is
communicated and made known in the persons of his saints, 'those
who are becoming united with God'.

One of the great images of this final blessedness is provided by
the sun itself with its life-giving light and warmth. 'Then shall the
righteous shine forth as the sun'; 'The sun of righteousness will arise,
with healing in his wings.' Commenting on the primordial place
amongst the creatures which the sun holds in St Francis's great Canticle, Leclerc speaks also of the inner sun, the great archetypal symbol of light which comes to life within him:

Francis is clothed with the sun . . . A symbol of the Most

High, and yet a brother. A sun at once sacred and yet close to us. Francis does not simply see this sun, with his enfeebled eyes, shining over the plain of Assisi. He experiences it with all his being. The great cosmic image rises from the depths of his being. It is the expression of an inner fulness.... In it, Francis' soul recognises and celebrates symbolically, although unconsciously, his own transfiguration, his own transformation in the Kingdom.... This marvellous substance of the sun, all of light, so brotherly yet marked with the seal of the Most High, is the unconscious, but infinitely expressive image of the soul which finds itself in the fulness of its energies and destiny, open to the whole of its mystery, reconciling in itself the lower and hidden powers of life and matter, with the awareness of its highest destiny and the radiant certainty of its divine calling.[16]

It is impossible to read this passage without thinking at once of Motovilov's description of the transfiguration of St Seraphim (though Leclerc makes no mention of it). The saint is speaking:

'Why then, my friend, do you not look me straight in the face? Look freely and without fear; the Lord is with us.'

Encouraged by these words, I looked and was seized by holy fear. Imagine in the middle of the sun, dazzling in the brilliance of its noontide rays, the face of the man who is speaking to you. You can see the movements of his lips, the changing expression of his eyes, you can hear his voice, you can feel his hands holding you by the shoulders, but you can see neither his hands nor his body — nothing except the blaze of light which shines around, lighting up with its brilliance the snow-covered meadow, and the snowflakes which continue to fall unceasingly.

'What do you feel?' asked Father Seraphim.

'An immeasurable well-being,' I replied.

'But what sort of well-being? What exactly?'

'I feel', I replied, 'such calm, such peace in my soul, that I can find no words to express it.'

'My friend, it is the peace our Lord spoke of when he said to his disciples: "My peace I give unto you," the peace which the world cannot give, "the peace which passes all understanding". What else do you feel?'

'Infinite joy in my heart.'

Father Seraphim continued: 'When the Spirit of God des-
cends on a man, and envelops him in the fullness of his presence,
the soul overflows with unspeakable joy, for the Holy Spirit fills
everything he touches with joy . . .' [17]

Indeed, when the Holy Spirit touches the whole of a man, energis-
ing and transforming his life at every level, a wonderful radiance of
glory is released.

It has often been said, it is said by Lossky himself, that whereas
the saints of the West are marked with the wounds of Christ, the
saints of the East are transfigured with the divine light; whereas the
one tradition concentrates its attention on the Cross, the other lives
in the light of the resurrection. Confronted with the figures of St
Francis and St Seraphim, such a contrast seems superficial and over-
simplified. What is evident in both is the manifestation of the joy
and peace of the Kingdom through the way of the Cross, which is
known as the life-giving Cross. What is evident in both is that at the
end of their lives the light of God shines out through the very body
of the one who has died with Christ so that he might live with
Christ. In both traditions death and resurrection are inseparably
linked together.

If we turn to the East, we find that the inner reality which the
stigmata outwardly seal and express is by no means unknown in
monastic tradition. The monk is one who can say in a particular
way, 'I am crucified with Christ,' one who bears 'in his body the
marks of the Lord Jesus'. We can see this in more recent centuries in
the frequently found icon which depicts the monk as fastened to the
Cross, subject to the attacks of the evil powers, identified with the
Lord in his sufferings for man. We can see this at an earlier time by
the way in which the calling of the pillar saints was understood.
Their strange way of life was an extreme expression of the principle
of monastic stability. In mounting the pillar, these men were mounting the Cross. We may remember even earlier the strange expressions in the Coptic life of St Pachomius which tell how a cherub
appeared to him, took the measure of his chest, and 'crucified him
on the earth', words which remind us directly of the story of St
Francis.[18]

In the case of St Seraphim, the thousand days and nights which he spent standing on a rock in the forest, crying 'Lord have mercy,' might be understood as his personal way of entering into this reality of the Cross. The fifteen years which he spent in total seclusion in his cell, not even seeing the face of the brother who brought him his meals, would then correspond to the reality of being buried with Christ. We read of the radiance of the old man as he greeted everyone who came to him during the last years of his life with the salutation of Easter, 'My joy, Christ is risen.' We sometimes forget the long, hard years of silence and solitude and physical toil which preceded them. Before the resurrection had come the tomb.

On the other hand, when we turn to St Francis we find always that the love of the crucified Lord, and the pain and grief of the knowledge of his passion, is mingled with the joy and the peace which comes from the resurrection. In his prayer on Mount Alverna, on the very eve of the stigmata, Francis prays for two things, first that he may know as far as is possible in his own body the pain which our Lord suffered for all mankind, and secondly that he may know, as far as is possible, in his heart, the love which moved him to bear it. The radiance which had accompanied Francis in the first years of his conversion does not desert him in the last two years of his life. Quite the reverse; though broken in health, nearly blinded by the disease in his eyes, suffering from the wounds in his hands and feet and side, it is in this period that he writes the Canticle of the Creatures, and fills all who come to him with the awareness of the presence of the Kingdom.

For here, precisely, the two saints are at one in their anticipation —here and now—of the fullness of the end of all things. In the vision which came before the composition of the Canticle of the Creatures, Francis sees the earth, as it were, transmuted into gold, and receives the assurance that already he is in possession of a greater treasure in sharing in the joy of the Kingdom of Heaven. While at the very heart of the conversation of Father Seraphim with Motovilov lies the affirmation that already they are in the Holy Spirit, and the Holy Spirit is in them. 'For the heart of a man is capable of containing the Kingdom of God. The Holy Spirit and the Kingdom of God are one,'[19] declares the saint. In both, the blessedness of the Kingdom is made known even in time. Through the brokenness of their bodies, the fullness and glory of the consummation of all things shines out.

St Benedict instructs us that the one who comes to enter the monastic brotherhood is to be asked 'whether he truly seeks God'. Here are two men who – following the way of the evangelical counsels – have not ceased to seek, and who have revealed in their lives something of that infinite capacity of the human heart for sorrow and for joy, for love and for understanding, which is made manifest if only we will give it up to God. Here are two men who reveal to us not only the deep underlying unity which joins together Churches canonically separated, but also the fact that such unity within the Church is inseparable from unity with all creation, and unity within the heart and mind of man. We need not fear, if we follow St Francis, that in estimating very highly the sacramental character of all created things, as he did, we shall undervalue the preciousness of the specific sacraments of the Church; on nothing does he insist more than on the honour which is due to the Eucharistic body of the Lord. But, again, in rating very highly the sacrament of the altar, we need not fear that we shall ignore the reality of the sacrament of our brother. The mysterious way in which the Lord comes to us in every man, and particularly in those who are despised and outcast, was experienced by Francis with an exceptional intensity. The social, personal, cosmic dimensions of reconciliation and unity are brought together in one.

And again, while we rightly celebrate the restoration of the monastic and religious order within our Church, we cannot but perceive in both St Francis and St Seraphim that the inner reality of the religious or monastic life overflows beyond the confines of the monastic institution. This surely is the meaning both of the calling of the Third Order, those who while living in the world are yet closely united in heart and mind with the Brothers and Sisters of the first two Orders, and of the way in which the First Order itself is sent out into the world. This surely also is part of the meaning of the fact that the conversation of St Seraphim is with a married layman, and that the saint assures him that their difference of outward status makes no difference to their common participation in the Kingdom of the Holy Trinity. Where the Spirit comes he brings unity, a unity which does not destroy but fulfils the diversity and richness of the world which God has made.

'The walls of separation do not reach up to heaven'; Metropolitan Platon of Kiev is evidently right. But, alas, they are still with us here on earth. The Churches to which St Francis and St Seraphim belonged have been out of communion with each other for nine hundred years. Over large areas and for long periods they have been divided by bitter hostility no less than by indifference and ignorance. Most of the faithful on one side of the divide are ignorant of the very existence of the saints of the other. Much of the official theology of both Greeks and Latins has denied the very possibility of holiness beyond the canonical boundaries of their Church. So strong has been the consciousness on both sides of the schism of the identity of the Church today with the Church before the schism, that in practice the existence of the other body as a real vehicle of God's saving power has been denied.

Nor should we as Anglicans congratulate ourselves over much on our part in this tragic situation. Over long periods since the Reformation, and in some places still today, it is rare enough to find any serious thought and concern about the restoration of unity, or any living consciousness of the presence of the saints with us, of their continuing intercession for us. We are, let us remember, a Church which is still not fully in communion with the great apostolic sees either of East or West, nor fully recognised by them. Nevertheless, in God's grace, the very fragility of our position, the fact that we cannot be tempted to suppose that we are the whole, gives us certain possibilities of openness to others which we should use to the full. As we have thought at the beginning of this essay, the movement which began in Oxford in 1833, the year St Seraphim died, involved not only a renewal of the sense of catholicity within our own Church, but an affirmation of the existence of an underlying unity between the separated branches of the Christian family and of the reality of the communion of saints across the barriers of death. The longing for unity which was born then, and the renewed consciousness of our fellowship with the saints, have not ceased to grow as the years have passed. We are perhaps as a Church in a privileged position which enables us to recognise not only privately but publicly the saints whom God has given to other bodies, and even now to commemorate liturgically the activity of the one Spirit, the presence of the one Lord, amongst those with whom we are not in canonical communion. In the various provinces of the Anglican Communion we have growing opportunities for the commemoration of those who have not previously been included in our official calendars. 'The walls of separation do not reach up to heaven.' By the grace of God they become less solid even here below.

There is then something that we can each of us do; not only in prayer, though primarily there. Each one of us in some measure, can make their own the prayer of Thomas Merton, to unite in himself the traditions of divided Christendom. Each one of us can come, quite simply, to love and to know the gifts of holiness which God has given to divided Christians even in their state of separation, and can rejoice more fully in the activity of 'the divine grace which always fills up what is lacking and heals what is wounded'. We can, furthermore, take whatever opportunities are given us for making contacts across the barriers existing now; contacts not only of social courtesy and politeness, but contacts at the level of prayer and the sharing of spiritual gifts, seeking to understand more of the way in which the one Spirit has led us in the times of mutual estrangement. Here again there is much to be done, and much that communities, monastic and religious, are particularly capable of doing.

And all this will be of little avail unless it is rooted in a genuine growth in the love and knowledge of God. So that all work for Christian unity must be rooted in the prayer for the coming of the Holy Spirit, that he will descend upon the offering of the Church transmuting our gifts into his gift, that he will descend upon the offering which each one makes in the holy and most secret place of his own heart and mind. We must pray that we may have his gift of wisdom as well as his gift of praise, so that through us there may be a renewal of the theology of prayer. Above all, that in his coming, the reconciling presence of the Kingdom of the Father, the Son, and the Holy Spirit may be revealed amongst men, and all things hasten to their joyful consummation.

NOTES

1. Quoted in M. Villain, *L'Abbé Paul Couturier, Apôtre de l'Unité Chrétienne* (Paris 1957) p. 51.

2. St Stephen of Muret quoted in Rose Graham, *English Ecclesiastical Studies* (London 1929) p. 212. I am grateful at this as at other points in this text to the suggestions of my friend, the Revd. James Coutts.

3. T. Merton, *Contemplation in a World of Action* (1972) p. 211.

4. Eloi Leclerc, *Le Cantique des Créatures ou les Symboles de l'Union* (Paris 1970) p. 200.

5. Ibid. p. 201.

6. A. J. Wensinck, *Mystic Treatises of Isaac of Nineveh* (Wiesbaden 1969). p. 8.

7. Thomas Traherne, *Poems, Centuries and Three Thanksgivings*, ed. Anne Ridler (London 1966) p. 177.

8. Leclerc, op. cit. p. 202.

9. Ibid.

10. Ibid. p. 197.

11. Ibid.

12. V. Lossky, *The Mystical Theology of the Eastern Church* pp. 110–11.

13. Ibid. p. 111.

14. 'The Mirror of Perfection', 118, *S. Francis of Assisi. Writings and Early Biographies*, ed. M. A. Habig (Chicago 1972) p. 1257.

15. II Celano, Cp. CXXIV, 165, *S. Francis of Assisi. Writings and Early Biographies* pp. 494–5.

16. Leclerc, op. cit. p. 86.

17. Lossky, op. cit. pp. 228–9.

18. See K. T. Ware in *Sacrament and Image*, ed. A. M. Allchin (London 1967) p. 21.

19. St Seraphim of Sarov, quoted in Irina Gorainov, *The Message of Saint Seraphim* (SLG Press, Oxford 1973) p. 14.

6

The Rebirth of Hope:

a study of Thomas Merton

The life of Thomas Merton was at first sight full of paradoxes, and Merton himself was fully aware of this fact. Here was a man who became a monk, entering the Cistercian monastery of Gethsemani, Kentucky, at the age of twenty-six, renouncing the world and in particular the literary ambitions which he had dearly cherished. Within a few years he had written a book describing his conversion which at once became a best-seller. He had sought to be unknown; he found himself famous.

As Merton went on in the monastic way, he entered more and more deeply into the life of his community; for some years he was novice-master. He read very extensively in the whole literature of Christian spirituality, both of East and West. In his books, and in his teaching given within the community, he re-expressed that tradition in terms which belong to our own unmonastic century. Finally in the last years of his life he withdrew into solitude. He lived in a hermitage in the woods above the monastery, near enough to be in constant contact with the community, but far enough away to have a greater degree of silence and solitariness than even the most silent and ordered of communities can provide. It was a life of monastic striving if ever there was one.

And yet at the end of his life it is hard to imagine a man more universal in his concerns, his interests, his friendships. He knew and loved people in every continent of our planet, and people in every part of the world knew and loved him, not only through his books, but also through correspondence and the visits which they made to him. 'A monk is one who is separated from all and united to all,' wrote Evagrius, one of the very first theoreticians of the monastic life. It was eminently true of Thomas Merton.

The life of Thomas Merton was at first sight full of paradoxes. His earlier writings, *Elected Silence, Seeds of Contemplation, The Ascent to Truth* were immensely popular in the early 1950s on both sides of the Atlantic. They expressed in terms of spirituality the mood of a somewhat triumphalist moment in British and American Catholicism, a moment symbolised at another level by *Brideshead Revisited*. It was, interestingly enough, Evelyn Waugh who wrote the introduction to the English edition of Merton's autobiography abridging it in order to make it more acceptable to the British reading public. It was a time which saw things in stark black and white. Everything within the Roman Catholic Church was good, within the monastic life superlatively good; everything outside from Marxism to the Church of England was bad, and probably irredeemably so. Merton never repudiated these early writings, but in his later years he sometimes felt annoyed at their continuing popularity, believing that he had outgrown the intolerant, rather superficial young man who had composed them. Then in the later fifties his popularity waned. He continued to write, but many of his books were never published on this side of the Atlantic, and those that were, were not easy to obtain. It was said that he had left the monastery, that he had become a Carthusian, that he had lost his faith, that he had become a communist, and finally that he had become a Buddhist (or was it a Buddha?) and that this was why he had died in Thailand.

Well, at least it is true that he died in Bangkok. He was there attending a conference of Christian monks and nuns, mostly drawn from communities in Asia. They were endeavouring to understand more clearly how the Christian monastic tradition may take root in that continent, which has its own ancient and flourishing indigenous forms of monastic life. Merton had been invited as one who within the monastic tradition was acknowledged as a master. He had come with the blessing and approval of his community and his abbot, making an extended journey away from Gethsemani for the first time in twenty-seven years. At the time of the meeting in Bangkok he had already visited Ceylon and India, making contacts above all, with men of monastic life both Buddhist and Hindu. He planned to go on to Japan where he was widely known through the translations of his writings, and where many friends, Buddhist and Christian, awaited him. He had thoughts of returning to America by way of Western Europe, taking in the British Isles in the course of his journey. But an encounter with a faulty electric fan brought this leg of his journey to an end. The electric shock caused a heart attack from which he died immediately. It was December 10th 1968.

How was the man who died on that December afternoon related to the man who exactly twenty-seven years earlier had entered the community at Gethsemani on December 10th 1941? Merton had been a more than ordinarily faithful and consistent monk. He had lived out his life within a single community, within a single place. He had followed his first dedication to the life of prayer with a remarkable perseverance. The one who comes to enter the monastic brotherhood is to be asked whether he truly seeks God. Merton had not ceased to seek. He had not ceased to grow. He had concentrated all his life into one point, and in and through that concentration he had found an indefinite expansion of life and understanding. The very last book which he completed, *The Climate of Monastic Prayer*, bears witness to the wisdom and the insight which he had achieved by the end of his not so very long life (he was fifty-three when he died). He no longer saw the power of evil as something altogether outside the Church, outside the believer. He knew that the struggle was more inward than that; that in ourselves the healing power of God must be at work to cure the world's sickness. He had left all things for God. But in finding God all things had been given back to him. The first movement had been necessary, the movement of resolute rejection of all that was in the world. But it was completed and fulfilled by a second movement, or a second stage of development in which the world was rediscovered as the world in which God is at work. By losing his life, he found it.

Just how true it was that *all* was given back to him, we shall hardly know until a full biography of him is complete and published. But already one can gain some idea of the spread of his interests. There was the great extent of his contacts with writers in North America and Europe (Pasternak for instance was one of his correspondents). He was one of the leading authorities in the United

States on Latin American poetry, both in Spanish and Portuguese; in his translations and his articles he reveals a sympathetic under-standing of the subject not often rivalled in the English-speaking world. There was the depth of his involvement with both the peace movement and the civil rights movement in the United States; all this apart from his many ecumenical contacts amongst Anglicans, Orthodox and Protestants. But there were .nany other sides of his interest and activity; above all his extensive work to promote a bet-ter understanding amongst Western readers of the contemplative traditions of the other religions, Buddhist, Hindu and Muslim, and his efforts to encourage a dialogue of prayer and mutual exchange between men of contemplation wherever they are to be found.

It was indeed astonishing that a man so wholly cut off geographically from the great centres of human life and activity should be so vitally in contact with so many areas of human con-cern. Of course all kinds of people came to see him: eminent Japanese authorities on Zen, people involved up to the hilt in the struggle for racial justice, students from the local Southern Baptist Seminary, Benedictine scholars from Europe, celebrities like Joan Baez. (Merton once remarked that one of the advantages of being a hermit was that you could sing while getting the breakfast, without disturbing anyone, except perhaps the frogs, and they could join in the chorus. When asked what he sang, he mentioned among other things 'Silver Dagger'.) 'A monk is one separated from all, and un-ited with all.' It certainly came true. Some words of Fr George Congreve, one of the first generation of Anglican religious in the nineteenth century, a disciple and companion of Fr Benson of Cowley, illuminate his position. 'The consecration of the Christian tends to a unity like that with which life can collect, hold together and fertilize innumerable atoms in any live organism. The con-secrated man has not fewer interests in life than another; he may have more, but how many soever they are, they do not divide, dis-tract, exhaust him, because he holds them all together, along with himself, by a vital link to God.' [1] Indeed it is from God himself that the act of consecration springs.

But it is of course to Merton's own writings that we should turn to gain a deeper understanding of the amazing fruitfulness of his life, of the way in which the movement of renunciation is a necessary, an indispensable condition for a movement of rediscovery, perhaps of transfiguration. Many clues are to be found in an essay called 'Notes for a Philosophy of Solitude', which appears in the collection *Disputed Questions*, first published in 1960. This essay marks something of a turning point in Merton's writing. Already the footnote to the title finds him wrestling with the problem of monasticism, finds him seeking to affirm his solidarity with all who find themselves to be solitary (and that in some sense, might in the end include all men). 'I am speaking of the solitary spirit which is really essential to the monastic view of life, but which is not confined to monasteries. Nor is it limited to men and women who have consecrated their lives to God by vow. Therefore, though I am treating of the traditional concept of the *monachos* or solitary, I am deliberately discarding everything that can conjure up the artificial image of the monk in cowl, dwelling in a medieval cloister.' [2] There is, he is saying, a true form of solitude, to be distinguished from its counterfeits. What are its characteristics?

'Withdrawal from other men can be a special form of love for them. It should never be a rejection of man or of his society. But it may well be a quiet and humble refusal to accept the myths and fictions with which social life cannot help but be full – especially today. To despair of the illusions and façades which man builds around himself is certainly not to despair of man. On the contrary, it may be a sign of love and hope. For when we love someone, we refuse to tolerate what destroys and maims his personality. If we love mankind, can we blind ourselves to man's predicament? You will say: we must do something about his predicament. But there are some whose vocation it is to realize, that they, at least, cannot help in any overt social way. Their contribution is a mute witness, a secret and even invisible expression of love which takes the form of their own option for solitude in preference to the acceptance of social fictions. . . . Such men, out of pity for the universe, out of loyalty to mankind, and without a spirit of bitterness or of resentment, withdraw into the healing silence of the wilderness, or of poverty, or of obscurity, not in order to preach to others, but to heal in themselves the wounds of the entire world.' [3]

For one of the things which the man of prayer discovers is that all men are one man, one man is all men. In each one of us 'the

wounds of the entire world' may be healed by the action of the
forgiving grace of God. The struggle between life and death, between hope and despair is carried on within us, as well as around us,
as we allow the power of Christ risen to be at work in the deep
places of our hearts and minds.

There is here a great discovery about the catholicity, the universality of the human person, on which Merton reflected much in the
later years of his life. The aim of the Christian's asceticism may be
described as the death of the individual, so that the true person may
be born; the individual, understood as the one who hugs his life to
himself, who lives by opposing himself to others, by seeking to
dominate or possess them; the person, understood as the one who
gives himself fully, and finds in so doing that he can only truly live
by giving and receiving, and that in a mysterious way he contains
the whole within himself. Merton saw this growth into wholeness in
relation to his own particular work for Christian unity. 'If I can unite *in myself* the thought and the devotion of Eastern and Western
Christendom, the Greek and the Latin Fathers, the Russian with the
Spanish mystics, I can prepare in myself the reunion of divided
Christians. From that secret and unspoken unity in myself can eventually come a visible and manifest unity of all Christians. . . . If I do
not have unity in myself, how can I even think, let alone speak, of
unity among Christians? Yet, of course, in seeking unity for all
Christians, I also attain unity within myself.' [4]

But this mystery of the human person extends even further. In
one of his last writings Merton speaks of it in terms of 'final integration'. 'The man who has attained final integration is no longer
limited by the culture in which he has grown up. . . . He accepts not
only his own community, his own society, his own friends, his own
culture, but all mankind. With this view of life, he is able to bring
perspective, liberty and spontaneity into the lives of others. The
finally integrated man is a peacemaker. . . .' [5] Taken by themselves
perhaps these words could sound abstract or unreal. Taken in connection with Merton as his friends knew him, they were simply true.
'Perspective, liberty, spontaneity', these were things which his
presence, his company conveyed, without anything necessarily very
momentous being said. There was in him that power which characterises true holiness, the power to liberate in others gifts which they

never knew they had. God was at work within him revealing both in him and in those who came into contact with him, the truly, universally human thing, that which makes man to be man, what theology terms 'the image and likeness of God'.

What at times Merton describes in calm reflective prose, is in other places described in terms of personal experience, and nowhere more vividly than in a passage in *Conjectures of a Guilty Bystander*, the third of his directly autobiographical books. 'In Louisville, at the corner of Fourth and Walnut, in the center of the shopping district, I was suddenly overwhelmed with the realization that I loved all those people, that they were mine and I theirs, that we could not be alien to one another even though we were total strangers. It was like waking from a dream of separateness, of spurious self-isolation in a special world, the world of renunciation and supposed holiness. The whole illusion of a separate holy existence is a dream. Not that I question the reality of my vocation, or of my monastic life; but the conception of "separation from the world" that we have in the monastery too easily presents itself as a complete illusion: the illusion that by making vows we become a different species of being, pseudo-angels, "spiritual men", men of interior life, what have you.

'Certainly these traditional values are very real, but their reality is not of an order outside everyday existence in a contingent world, nor does it entitle one to despise the secular: though "out of the world" we are in the same world as everyone else, the world of the bomb, the world of race hatred, the world of technology, the world of mass media, big business, revolution, the rest. We take a different attitude to all these things, for we belong to God. Yet so does everybody else belong to God. We just happen to be conscious of it, and to make a profession out of this consciousness. But does that entitle us to consider ourselves different, or even *better* than others? The whole idea is preposterous.

'This sense of liberation from an illusory difference was such a relief and such a joy to me that I almost laughed out loud. And I suppose my happiness could have taken form in the words: "Thank God, thank God that I *am* like other men, that I am only a man among others.".... It is a glorious destiny to be a member of the human race. A member of the human race! To think that such a commonplace realisation should seem like news that one holds the winning ticket in a cosmic sweepstake.' [6]

Such a moment of awareness is a gift, a gift which we may suspect is not unrelated to the long years of discipline which have preceded it, and which have in some way prepared the seer to receive it. The years of strict asceticism were not irrelevant to the final vision. They were its necessary pre-condition. But they were not an end in themselves. There is throughout the Christian life, and particularly in the life of prayer, this strange and mysterious relationship between man's effort and God's gift. All is of grace, yet we cannot receive it unless we freely and wholeheartedly respond. How shall we find, unless we seek? How shall it be opened, unless we knock?

For a man of Merton's vehement and whole-hearted temperament there was perhaps a tendency to try too hard, and to try in the wrong way. There was also the temptation, particularly strong in the United States, to measure prayer and sacrifice in terms of quantity and outward efficiency. One suspects that there was a moment of crisis in his life when he began to realise that it is through accepting one's limitation, one's brokenness, that one can grow further into the way of love and understanding. 'Maybe the hermit turns out, unaccountably, to have his ulcer like the next man. No doubt he has to drink large quantities of milk and perhaps take medicines. This finally disposes of any hope of his becoming a legendary figure. He, too, worries. Perhaps he worries even more than the others, for it is only in the minds of those who know nothing about it that the solitary life appears to be a life free from all care.' [7] The man of prayer and faith must be careful not to measure himself against the world's standards of success. 'The monk is compassionate in proportion as he is less practical and less successful, because the job of being a success in a competitive society leaves one no time for compassion.'[8]

The note of compassion is more and more strongly heard in these later writings of Merton. His own constant activity as a writer was surely an expression of his compassionate love for his fellow human beings, an overflow of his desire to share with them something of what he had been given through his years of silence and renunciation. He had the powerful conviction, common to all the great representatives of the tradition of Christian spirituality, that what he was given was not for himself alone, but for all who could and would hear. He was by natural gift a writer, one whose business is with words. He felt all the more acutely the innumerable ways in which words are threatened and destroyed in our society. He knew too the healing power of silence, and the necessary dialectic which there is between speech and silence. 'For language to have meaning, there must be intervals of silence somewhere to divide word from word, and utterance from utterance. He who retires into silence does not necessarily hate language. Perhaps it is love and respect for language which impose silence upon him. For the mercy of God is not heard in words unless it is heard, both before and after the words are spoken, in silence.' [9] Anyone who has noticed the quality which words receive when spoken out of silence, whether in a time of retreat, or in the setting of a monastic community will recognise the truth of this statement. But, of course, it has wider and further implications.

And linked with this note of compassion is a note of a great and apparently inexplicable hope. This is expressed very movingly in *Conjectures* in a passage where Merton, doing the rounds of the monastery night watch, passes through the novitiate room, and pauses to reflect on his own experience as novice master and on his contacts with those who have been under his tuition. 'The loveliness of the humanity which God has taken to himself in love is, after all, to be seen in the humanity of our friends, our children, our brothers, the people we love and who love us. Now that God has become incarnate, why do we go to such lengths all the time, to "disincarnate" him again ? . . . You can see the beauty of Christ in each individual person, in that which is most his, most human, most personal to him. . . . In any case, I felt there was something quite final and eternal in looking at this empty room: that though they themselves might not understand what they are going through, and though many of them may fail, may leave, or may have to look elsewhere to get the real meaning of their lives, yet the sign of love is on these novices and they are precious for ever in God's eyes. Certainly it has been a great gift of his love to me, that I am their novice master. It is very good to have loved these people and been loved by them with such simplicity and sincerity, within our ordinary limitation, without nonsense, without flattery, without sentimentality, and without getting too involved in one another's business.'[10]

And from this basic experience of the possibility of growth in love and knowledge and understanding within the monastic community, Merton goes on to reflect that it may be possible to recover hope even for the political dimension of man's life, which may often seems so intractably hopeless. Man *can* live at peace with his brother, *can* live at peace with himself, when he is truly seeking to receive the peace of God. It is not so easy to do nor indeed so pious as it sounds when set out in traditional language, but, because there is love in the world, and because Christ has taken our nature to himself, there remains always the hope that man can find the way of peace, which alone is the way of life for him.

This sense of the peace which comes from God as a gift which we can receive, and even in some measure, hand on, pervades Merton's later books. It finds expression in a passage in *Conjectures* entitled 'A Prayer to God the Father on the Vigil of Pentecost', a passage which seems to me to be amongst the finest that he ever wrote, part of which is cited here.

'Whatever may have been my particular stupidity, the prayers of your friends and my own prayers have somehow been answered, and I am here, in this solitude, before you, and I am glad because you see me here. For it is here, I think, that you want to see me and I am seen by you. My being here is a response you have asked of me, to something I have not clearly heard. But I have responded, and I am content: there is little more to know about it at present.

'Here you ask of me nothing else than to be content that I am your child and your friend. Which means simply to accept your friendship because it is your friendship and your Fatherhood because I am your son. This friendship is Sonship, and is Spirit. You have called me here to be repeatedly born in the Spirit as your son. Repeatedly born in light, in knowledge, in unknowing, in faith, in awareness, in gratitude, in poverty, in presence, and in praise.

'If I have any choice to make, it is to live here and perhaps to die here. But in any case it is not the living or the dying that matter, but speaking your name with confidence in this light, in this unvisited place; to speak your name of "Father" just by being here as "son" in

the Spirit and the Light which you have given, and which are no un-
earthly light but simply this plain June day, with its shining fields,
its tulip trees, the pines, the woods, the clouds, and the flowers
everywhere.

'To be here with the silence of Sonship in my heart is to be a center in which all things converge upon you. This is surely enough for
the time being.

'Therefore, Father, I beg you to keep me in this silence so that I
may learn from it the word of your peace, and the word of your
mercy and the word of your gentleness to the world: and that
through me perhaps your word of peace may make itself heard
where it has not been possible for anyone to hear it for a long time.

'To study truth here and learn here to suffer for truth.

'The Light itself, and the contentment and the Spirit, these are
enough.

'Amen.' [11]

Jean Leclercq, one of the foremost monastic scholars of our time,
in his introduction to the posthumous collection of Merton's articles
on contemplative questions, *Contemplation in a World of Action*,
writes 'I am not giving way to an ingenuous, admiring expression of
friendship when I rank Merton with the Fathers of the Early
Church, and those of the Middle Ages.' [12] If we would seek for a
spiritual guide for our own century, we could hardly find a better
one than him, a man who was profoundly rooted in the great tradition of Christian prayer and spirituality, common to East and West
alike, and was yet at the same time, in so many unexpected ways, so
wholly a man of our own times. In him the classical themes of
Christian prayer and reflection came to life, and were experienced
anew. The monastic life ceased to be a venerable and impressive
relic from the past, and became a living and creative power, now.
The essential need of the human person both for solitude and communion was vividly exemplified in his life and activity. Both by
what he wrote and by what he was he pointed forward to a new
discovery of that which truly makes men one, their common sonship
of the one Father, their common participation in the one and life-
giving Spirit. Of all the photographs which were taken of him,
perhaps none is more eloquent than that taken with the Dalai Lama
at the end of their third long conversation. Two men of prayer,

from two wholly different traditions, they had found in one another an unlooked for realisation of a common mystery, a shared experience.

Like many prophetic figures, it is probable that his greatest influence is yet to come. The first period of the popularity of his early writings, after a decade of comparative neglect has been followed by a new and fuller rediscovery of his works. More and more are being re-published and explored. The years that have followed his death have revealed ever more sharply the fundamental flaws in the political, social and economic life of our North American — Western European world, which he so clearly saw and diagnosed throughout his writings. The importance of his witness can be recognised afresh as the need for a rediscovery of the contemplative dimension of life is coming to be much more widely acknowledged. Attempts to recover valid forms of community life, and to explore the inner ways of prayer and meditation abound, though more outside the Church than within it. Such efforts need the traditional wisdom and balance which the masters of the spiritual life can provide. The Church desperately needs the enthusiasm and devotion which in many cases fail to find a lasting and creative form in which to develop. We shall find, if we will only attend, a word of liberation and a word of hope in the writing and life of one who by all that he was and by all that he did testified to the fact that the vision of God is the only true life of man, and that the glory of God is revealed in man fully alive.

NOTES

1. George Congreve, *Christian Progress and Other Essays* (1913) pp. 144–5.
2. Thomas Merton, *Disputed Questions* (1960) p. 177.
3. ibid. pp. 192–4.
4. Thomas Merton, *Conjectures of a Guilty Bystander* (1966) p. 12 and p. 128.
5. Thomas Merton, *Contemplation in a World of Action* (1971) p. 212.
6. *Conjectures*, pp. 140–1.
7. *Disputed Questions* p. 201.
8. ibid. p. 200.

9. ibid. p. 195.
10. *Conjectures* p. 194.
11. ibid. pp. 160–1.
12. *Contemplation* p. xx.

The Way of Solitude

some theological considerations

The question to be discussed in this chapter is one of vital importance not only for the whole Church, but for all mankind, even though it centres on a way of life which, in our time at least, seems particularly marginal. Yet, as I shall hope to suggest, the place of the solitary is only in appearance at the edge; in reality he is the one who stands at the very heart of things.

I am concerned here primarily with the theological aspect of the subject, but perhaps at the outset I may make a few very tentative preliminary remarks in relation to the historical and practical aspects of the matter. Historically it would seem that the solitary life has had an absolutely central place within the tradition of the Church, once we free ourselves from thinking that the last four centuries of Western Christian history (Protestant and Catholic) are normative for our view of the whole. Looking at the historical dimension of the question one is struck by two things: the importance of the hermit call through the Christian centuries; and the immense variety of ways in which the life has been led, and in which the solitary has been related to the Church as a whole, and to the monastic community in particular.

For if we may come to the more practical and pastoral approach to the question, there are, I think, three elementary points which I should like to make.

First: The life is one which demands considerable maturity, human and psychological, as well as ascetic and spiritual. It is not a way to be undertaken unadvisedly, lightly, or wantonly, and it will not ordinarily be undertaken without some considerable experience of a regular life of prayer and obedience lived in community.

Second: this is the recognition that the life is one which has particular dangers, and which demands considerable capacities of spiritual discernment both in those who follow this way and in those who seek to guide them.

Third: again, related to this is the vital recognition that each solitary is different. By the very nature of the calling there is something unique about each one. There are an indefinitely large number of ways of living the solitary life. This does not mean that there are no general principles underlying the life, nor does it mean that it will not be possible to discern a number of basic patterns of solitary life, largely measured by the degree of solitude involved and the forms of continuing association with the common life. It does mean, however, that it will be very difficult, indeed impossible, ever to legislate for and codify this way of life in a complete and systematic manner. Canon Lawyers must always admit themselves to some degree baffled at this point. Their categories will not finally be sufficient. And this fact is not an accident. It comes from the very nature of the vocation itself. And this brings us naturally to the main part of our discussion.

1

Let us begin with our view of the nature of man. The world in which we live brings great pressure upon us to think of human beings as units, numbers, replaceable and quantifiable. The whole technological and bureaucratic development of our society works in this direction. As machines become more and more important in human life, so more and more men are tempted to think of themselves in terms of cogs in a machine. This way of thinking of men and women as disposable units is not particularly new. We may suppose it to be characteristic of most previous human societies which were founded on slavery. But in our own times, which are in some ways freer, and which pride themselves on recognising true human dignity, it takes new, less obvious and even more oppressive forms. Faced with this situation men think of themselves as individuals, parts of the whole, who have to assert their individuality over against the whole.

Such a view of man makes any deep understanding of Christian faith and prayer and life impossible. For God's disclosure of himself in Christ and in the Spirit reveals to us not only the true nature of God, but also the true nature of man, made in God's image and likeness, personal and not individual. This distinction between person and individual has acquired particular importance in Christian thinking during the last hundred years. By man conceived as an individual, we refer to man conceived of as a small part of the whole, man who lives and survives by asserting himself against others, a creature who must either devour or be devoured. He can only become himself by separating himself from others; he can only become himself at the cost of others. This view of man was already propounded by Hobbes with great force in the seventeenth century. As a description of many of the features of fallen humanity, it has an unpleasant accuracy. As a description of the nature of man as created by God it is utterly false. For man is not an individual but a person. Not a replaceable part of the whole, but a unique and unrepeatable being in whom the whole (all humanity and indeed all creation) is mysteriously present. Man lives and survives not by asserting his own self against others, but by finding himself in and through others ('your brother is your life'). In freely giving himself to others he is not lost but renewed. He can only become himself in relationship to others, and far from this process of 'becoming himself' being at the expense of others, it is most profoundly with and for all others. In so far as the true nature of man, the image and likeness of God, is being restored in anyone, just so far it is potentially being restored in all.

This view of man derives, of course, from a reflection on the mystery of God's self-revelation in Christ, and on the co-inherence of the persons within the life of the Godhead, and it is a vital presupposition for any living of the solitary life. A person is one who recognises the unity of his nature with that of all men. We can only grow into the uniqueness of our personal being by recognising this common nature which we share. 'When thou seest the naked cover him, and hide not thyself from thine own flesh', says the prophet

Isaiah. 'Whoever debases another debases himself,' says a contemporary writer, James Baldwin. And the second great commandment is, of course, 'Thou shalt love thy neighbour as thyself.' And to love in this context means not to desire to dominate and possess, but to be willing to give oneself to the uttermost. This understanding of nature and person therefore is not a mere abstraction but a necessary tool for Christian living and praying, and it comes to us from our reflection on the very life of God in Trinity. The idea of a union which does not destroy the unique qualities of the beings united but brings them to perfection in uniting them comes from a reflection on the union of human and divine in Christ. And these considerations are essential for our view of the relation of each member of the Church to the Church as a whole. We shall never begin to understand the Church if we are thinking in terms of individuals and corporations. The Church is not an agglomeration of individuals – 'a sandheap of individual perfections', in Father Congreve's words – but a unity of persons, the fellowship of the Holy Spirit. In the Church, as in the divine nature itself, the opposition of the one and the many is overcome, for the Church is the place within the creation where the image of the Trinity is reflected, the place where man is restored in his true nature in God's image and likeness. There are many persons but one body, many gifts but one Spirit, and the gifts are not divided out separately to each, but what belongs to each is common to all, and what is common to all belongs to each.

Such a vision of the Church, I repeat, is vital for the living of the solitary life. Without it the life of solitude would be a madness, or a kind of ultimate solipsism. But at the same time, without the life of solitude lived, and indeed understood within the body of the Church, it will become increasingly difficult for the Church to retain this sense of her own nature. I do not know whether the comparative eclipse of the solitary life in Western Christendom was due to a comparable atrophying of this vision, or whether it was the decay of vision which followed on the obscuring of the way of life. I suspect that a study of history might show that it was the first and not the second. But what is clear already is that the two things go together. In our own century the recovery of the solitary life is profoundly linked with a number of other and at first sight apparently unrelated movements: liturgical, ecclesiological, and ecumenical which has revitalised the sense of the Church as a Communion of Life.

We can illustrate the points which have been made from the work of a Western writer whose thought reflects faithfully the tradition of the Church in the centuries before the schism of East and West. St Peter Damian's 'Book on the Lord be With You' was written in answer to certain hermits who had enquired whether they might use the salutation, 'The Lord be with you', when saying the Office alone. Damian replies that they may:

> Indeed, the Church of Christ is united in all her parts by such a bond of love that her several members form a single body and in each one the whole Church is mystically present, so that the whole Church Universal may rightly be called the one Bride of Christ, and on the other hand every single soul can, because of the mystical effect of the Sacrament, be regarded as the whole Church.[1]

In his reading of the Bible, Peter Damian had noticed something which has attracted the attention of many modern biblical exegetes: the identification of the whole people with one man is so strong that the one may stand for the whole people.

> If we look carefully through the fields of Holy Scripture we will find that one man or one woman often represents the whole Church, for though because of the multitude of her peoples the Church seems to be of many parts [note the recognition of a plurality of peoples within the Church's unity], yet she is nevertheless one and simple in the mystical unity of one faith and one divine baptism. For indeed, although holy Church is divided in the multiplicity of her members, yet she is fused into unity by the fire of the Holy Spirit, and so even if she seems, as far as her situation in the world is concerned, to be scattered, yet the mystery of her inward unity can never be marred in its integrity. 'The love of God is shed abroad in our hearts by the Holy Ghost which is given unto us.' This Spirit is without doubt both one and manifold, one in the essence of his greatness and manifold in the diverse gifts of his grace, and he gives to holy Church, which he

fills, this power that all her parts shall form a single whole, and that each part shall contain the whole. This mystery of undivided unity was asked for by Truth himself when he said to his Father concerning his disciples, 'I do not pray for them alone but for them also who shall believe in me through their word, that they all may be one as thou Father art in me and I in thee, that they also may be one in us that the world may believe that thou hast sent me.' [2]

Here is a vision of the Church, personal, sacramental and Trinitarian; a viewpoint full of consequence for our understanding of the element of multiplicity as well as the element of unity within the *Catholica*. We can see a close resemblance to that kind of eucharistic ecclesiology, developed in our own time by a number of Orthodox theologians, which insists on the fullness of each local church, united around its bishop, each one having in itself the wholeness of the Church's life, not being merely a part of the whole. But it is not only in each local church that the whole Church may be said to be present: it is in each member of the Church.

By the mystery of her inward unity the whole Church is spiritually present in the person of each human being who has a share in her faith and her brotherly love ... Indeed, if we who are many are one in Christ, each of us possesses in him the whole, and though in our bodily solitude we seem to be far from the Church, yet we are most immediately present in her through the invisible mystery of her unity. And so it is that that which belongs to all belongs to each, and conversely that which is particular to some is common to all in the unity of faith and love ... Now just as the Greeks call man a microcosm, that is to say, a little world, because his body is composed of the same four elements as the universe itself, so each of the faithful is a little Church since without violation of the mystery of her inward unity, each man receives all the sacraments of human redemption which are divinely given within the Church. [3]

If in Protestant theology (I do not say Protestant practice, for certainly in practice the solitary life has been and is lived within

Protestantism) the hermit life has scarcely been envisaged, it is because this vision of the Church's nature has been generally absent. And if in Roman Catholicism since the sixteenth century, the hermit way has been less in evidence than hitherto, and hardly recognised in canon law, may it not be in part because such a vision of the Church, in which each member shares in all the sacraments of human redemption (baptism, confirmation, and eucharist), has been overshadowed by other more juridical, clerical, and organisational views of the Church, forged in the heat of sixteenth-and seventeenth-century controversy? As long as the Church is conceived primarily in legal or institutional terms the solitary life will always appear as a threat to its unity and cohesion. The one will be thought of in contrast to the many, the solitary in contrast to the group. Only on the sacramental and personal view of things outlined here it is possible to see the co-inherence of the two contrasting realities, to see the solitary as expressing the inward unity of the community.

We see here one of the many ecumenical significances of the solitary way; not only because it unites us all in a common adherence to a vision of God, man and the Church which was the shared heritage of the first thousand years of Church history, but still more because the hermit by his very life and call, lives the unity of the Church in a strikingly vivid and genuine way. 'A Christian hermit can, by being alone, paradoxically live even closer to the heart of the Church than one who is in the midst of her apostolic activities,' writes one of the prophets of the eremitic renewal of our own day, Thomas Merton. 'Perhaps none have realised as intensely the saving mystery of fellowship, the love of brethren, as those whom God has called to live by prayer in the greatest solitude, even in the continual contemplation of the hermit,' wrote one who was amongst the first theologians of the Anglican revival of the Religious Life in the nineteenth century, George Congreve. Those who appear marginal are in reality central. They live a form of life whose very meaning is an affirmation of unity. They live it in Churches which for many centuries have not been in canonical communion with one another. The particular poignancy of this situation is heightened when we remember the great role that the Churches which did not accept the decisions of Chalcedon had in the foundations of Christian monasticism, and when we recall that to this day, at least in Egypt and Ethiopia, this tradition of solitary life is still flourishing amongst them.

When we reflect how deep the influence of St Isaac of Syria on the spiritual tradition of Greece, Romania and Russia has been, we see something of the strangeness of this story. For the writer in question, one of the great exponents of the meaning of the solitary way was a bishop in the Nestorian Church, a Church for many centuries considered schismatic and heretical by the greater part of the Christian world. The divisions within Christendom are not of the last five or ten centuries alone. They go back into the first ages of the Church's life, and their meaning is perhaps different from what we usually take it to be.

2

So far we have spoken of the solitary life in terms of man's creation by God in his image and likeness. And though this line of thought has not been developed at length, underlying our whole discussion has been the faith that it is not only mankind which is involved in this creative work, but the whole universe. The cosmic dimension of prayer and life is very strongly developed in the solitary tradition, expressing itself in many ways, not least in a particular closeness to the animal creation.

But the meaning of this way of life is to be apprehended not only in terms of God's purpose in creation. Its full significance begins to become apparent when we see it in relation to the work of redemption, when we begin to understand it in terms of the Cross and the empty tomb. The solitary life is not only characterised by the quiet of the sabbath. It involves the single-handed conflict with the powers of evil, the way of the Cross, which necessarily precedes entry into the peace of God.

I should like to quote from one of the last utterances of Derwas Chitty, a talk he gave a few months before his death.[4] Fr Derwas saw the hermit as in some sense representative of us all. He spoke in images rather than concepts. He evoked the two places which meant most to him on this earth, Bardsey Island off the tip of the Lleyn Peninsula, in Wales, and the Church of the Holy Sepulchre in

Jerusalem, both of them places of meeting between man and God, both of them places of death and resurrection, both of them places where we find ourselves alone yet not alone.

First, the island of the saints: 'the island of hermits. The island of the solitude where one is least alone'. 'Each one who comes there seems immediately to make it his or her own. You don't need anyone else with you; you each do it in your own way. Everyone in a different way. But there you are.' And this which is perhaps true of every island was specially true of this island where through the centuries men longed to be buried to await there the day of judgement. This understanding of the meaning of Bardsey is something which finds expression more than once in medieval poetry, and most significantly in the last section of a poem of Meilyr Brydydd.

> May I, the poet Meilyr, pilgrim to Peter,
> Gatekeeper who judges the sum of virtue,
> When the time comes for us to arise
> Who are in the grave, make myself ready.
> May I be at home awaiting the summons
> In a fold with the moving sea near it,
> A desert it is of unfading honour
> With a bosom of brine about its graves
> Fair Mary's isle, pure island of the pure,
> The heir of resurrection, it is good to be in it.
> Christ of the foretold cross knows me, will keep me
> From the pains of hell, that place of exile.
> The Creator who created me will meet me
> In the fair parish of Enlli's faithful. [5]

These lines, which were very familiar to Fr Derwas, come from a deathbed poem of repentance and supplication written in the first half of the twelfth century. There are many things in them which demand our attention. First, how 'the fair parish of Enlli', namely, Bardsey Island, now geographically remote, was then near the centre of things. Meilyr was court poet to Gruffudd ap Cynan, a prince of Gwynedd who after many years of exile in Ireland managed to re-establish himself in North Wales. It has traditionally been thought that he brought back with him from Ireland strong influences in the realm of literature. Certainly his reign coincides with the beginning of the second major period of Welsh poetry. In such an Irish-Welsh perspective Bardsey, though always difficult of access, lies close to the principal routes between the two islands.

Then we must notice that these lines, so full of insight into the meaning of a holy place, are the work of one who was primarily a poet of war and love, one who praised the prowess of the prince's warriors, and the beauties of the ladies of the court. He was a man at the centre of his own small world. His son Gwalchmai ap Meilyr, and his grandson Einion ap Gwalchmai, succeeded him as court poets, and in the last named we find another poem containing a prayer to be buried on Bardsey. We have here a reflection of the attitudes of a whole society.

What is it that Meilyr sees about the meaning of the island? First it is a place of seclusion. The word translated 'desert', in the original *ditrif*, is one of the regular terms used in medieval Welsh for the dwelling of a hermit. And yet at the same time, the island is a place of assembly, of coming together, a place where one who is facing the solitude of death is supported by the communion of Mary and the saints. 'The island of solitude where one is least alone.' It is 'in the fair parish of Enlli's faithful', that he is to meet God. The use of the word parish (*plwyf*) is striking for the assembly of a monastic island, so closely are monk and layman associated in this vision of things, in this *solitudo pluralis*. Then, secondly, the island which is a place of death and burial, is at the same time the place of resurrection. Here we have one of the most remarkable and daring images in the poem. Having spoken of the island as Mary's isle, 'the pure island of the pure' (the word for 'pure' could equally well be translated 'holy'), he goes on to speak of it as 'the heir of resurrection' (*gwrthrych dadwyrein*). The word *gwrthrych*, which ordinarily means 'object' in Welsh, is used here in a technical sense to be found in old Welsh law to describe the heir to a king designated during his predecessor's lifetime. It may mean either 'the one who is in expectation' or 'the one who is expected'. In this case it would seem to be the former meaning which is the more appropriate. The island itself is in eager expectation of the resurrection of those who sleep within it.[6] All this, consciously or perhaps unconsciously, lay behind Fr Derwas's feeling for Bardsey.

And then the Church of the Holy Sepulchre in Jerusalem. Fr Derwas spoke of his many, almost daily, visits there when as a young man he was living in the holy city, unconsciously revealing something of the intense concentration of his own life on the person of the crucified and risen Lord.

Very early I tried to make a practice of going for a short time to the holy places each day. I did not manage it ... But, thank God, at least I tried to. Up on to that dark little Chapel which is Calvary. I would be there for quite a long time, going up and under the altar of Calvary and placing my arm through the hole in the plate underneath it to touch the bare rock on which the Cross had been set ... A longer time generally on Calvary, and then a shorter moment going into the Sepulchre, the place of Resurrection, which is the central point, the key point of that church, where it comes as such a shock in a way for a westerner to find that Calvary is on one side, and the centre is the tomb. And we go and call it the Church of the Holy Sepulchre. But in the Greek it is the Church of the Resurrection, the reason why, indeed, the Sepulchre is at the centre, the place of Easter.

I have quoted at some length because the specific quality of the original needs to be savoured. It is all so factual, yet so universal. Bardsey, an actual place; Calvary, an actual place. 'Placing my arm through the hole' — both places of death and resurrection, both places of solitude and communion.

And to speak of the Cross. The Lord has moved among men. He has suffered, he has done his works of mercy. But where do you and I meet him? There, in those first words upon the Cross when he is looking out on those around him, 'Father, forgive them, for they know not what they do.' 'Today shalt thou be with me in Paradise.' 'Woman, behold thy son.' 'Behold thy mother.' It is after these that the darkness over all the land speaks of the soul of Christ going down into the depths of darkness and loneliness, utterly alone: 'My God, my God, why hast thou forsaken me?' In that word we find him closest to us, and know him to be God.

Here we find the paradox of *solitudo pluralis* at its starkest. In the hour of desolation, the Lord is nearest to us and to all men.

Then, having evoked the experience of the risen Christ as he has made himself known through the centuries of the Church's history from the apostles until today, Fr Derwas went on to make the link between the Cross, the tomb, and each Christian — indeed each man — in his solitude before God, explicit by a reference to the pillar saints of Syria, men who adopted one of the most scandalous and public forms of solitary life ever to be known in this world. 'The pillar of one who is as fixed to his place of prayer as the Lord is fixed to the Cross, and there is no going back.' And that mounting of the pillar was itself understood as a mounting of the Cross, 'after all the training . . . of the life in common, the entry into the quiet of that solitude'. So, through the conflict, we pass in the power of the Cross into the quiet of the tomb, the place of new life. And out of this identification with 'the Christ upon the Cross, the Christ in the darkness, the Christ in the loneliness', there comes paradoxically but at once a new discovery of our fellow men.

What is the nearest way from me to my brother? The closest of human attachments must always recognise, if it is honest, the clear line of separation which sets the boundary between two souls . . . But there is a shorter way from my soul to my brother's. The Christ by his Holy Spirit is in the innermost shrine of your heart and mine. There, where I do not penetrate, in that Holy of Holies, where the Holy Spirit is enthroned in our baptism, there he is. And when we reach him there, we are closer to every soul of our brothers than we can be in any other way . . . And when we are serving our brothers and sisters in everyday life, there is something missing in our way of doing it unless somewhere at the roots of our being there is that prayer which turns inward to the Christ and finds him there, and by doing so, we are enabled to look out and see them and see the Christ in them, and see the Christ looking in upon us through the eyes of those around us. Not only those who are outwardly and consciously Christian, but everyone whom he loves . . .

So it is that in our own time the life of the hermit in some way

makes present to us the supreme paradox that it is in the moment of ⎫
utmost isolation and complete apparent uselessness, in the desolation ⎪
of the Cross, that the Lord is able to bring about the atonement and ⎬
reconciliation of man with God. That it is when he is lying dead in ⎭
the tomb that 'all creation is moving in him'. We are reminded of
the word of the Lord to Staretz Silouan, 'Keep your mind in hell
and despair not.' We are reminded of the apparent utter failure of
Charles de Foucauld dying in his desert hermitage, and of the way
in which life has come forth from that tomb. We are reminded in
our own Anglican tradition of the strange parallel in the life of Fr
William of Glasshampton. All that St Paul says about our dying
and rising with Christ, our union with him in his death no less than
in his resurrection, which is true for every Christian – in some sense,
indeed, for every human being – is true in their specific measure for
those who are called into the particular confinement of this narrow
way. The Cross is outside the city, the tomb is in a hidden garden;
but indeed they are at the true centre of the world.

3

We have considered the solitary life in relation to man's creation in
the image and likeness of God, and his redemption through the
death and resurrection of Christ. We must now come to consider
our subject in relation to the work of the Holy Spirit, in his coming
into the world at Pentecost. We have already had a clue as to this
action of the Holy Spirit in the passage which was quoted from
Peter Damian:

> For indeed, although holy Church is divided in the multiplicity of
> her members, yet she is fused into unity by the fire of the Holy
> Spirit ... This Spirit is without doubt both one and manifold,
> one in the essence of his greatness and manifold in the diverse
> gifts of his grace, and he gives to holy Church which he fills, this
> power that all her parts shall form a single whole, and that each
> part shall contain the whole.

There is within the Church a principle of unity and a principle of diversity or, we may say, a unity of nature expressed in a diversity of persons. The unity which the Spirit brings is not one which suppresses the true diversity of gifts, abolishing the uniqueness of each human person. Precisely the reverse is true: it is in the gift of the Spirit freely imparted and received that each one is established in the uniqueness of his own particular way. Amongst contemporary theologians few have written more illuminatingly on this subject than Vladimir Lossky, and though we need not commit ourselves to every detail of how he works out the relationship between the economy of the Son and the economy of the Spirit in the Church, we can certainly learn from the balance and insight with which he treats the matter.

Lossky presupposes the kind of distinction between personal and individual which we have already made:

> In the measure in which he is a person in the true theological sense of the word, a human being is not limited by his individual nature. He is not only a part of the whole, but potentially includes the whole, having in himself the whole earthly cosmos, of which he is the hypostasis. Thus each person is an absolutely original and unique aspect of the nature common to all. [7]

And it is precisely in relation to man's personal response to the word of God which calls him into being from nothing that this uniqueness needs to be stressed. We become the true and unique persons we are created to be, not in any attempt to assert ourselves or maintain ourselves by ourselves, but by going out of ourselves in love to God. For, says Lossky, 'it would appear that there are as many unions with God as there are human persons, each person having an absolutely unique relation with the Divinity . . .' [8] And it is the work of the Holy Spirit, who gives different gifts to each, to realise in each this unique calling.

> If our individual natures are incorporated into the glorious humanity of Christ and enter into the unity of his Body by baptism, conforming themselves to the death and resurrection of Christ, our persons need to be confirmed in their personal dignity by the Holy Spirit so that each may freely realise his own union

with the Divinity. Baptism — the sacrament of unity in Christ — needs to be completed by chrismation — the sacrament of diversity in the Holy Spirit. [9]

The relevance of this to the life of solitude is not far to seek. The one who is called to such a life needs to be one, above all, who is realising this personal vocation, realising, that is, both the profound unity and solidarity of all those who share in the body of Christ, and at the same time the extreme diversity of response called for by the grace of the Spirit which works in many ways and at many different levels. Speaking of the Church's awareness of the truth which it confesses, Lossky insists that this is not 'a "supra-consciousness" belonging to a collective person'. Rather, he maintains, 'there will necessarily be a multiplicity of consciousnesses, with different degrees of actualisation in different persons, more intensive in some, practically absent in others. Persons who are more deeply rooted in the Church, conscious of the unity of all in the Body of Christ, thus are more free of their own individual limitations, and their personal consciousness is more open to the Truth.' [10] Hence it may be in a moment of crisis for the Church, that the faith of the whole, the Catholic faith, will be realised in the *one*, an Athanasius or a Maximus, who has to stand against the overwhelming majority who have become blind to the truth.

To say that the call to the solitary life is a gift of the Holy Spirit in the Church is to say very little and yet to say everything. For in the coming of the Spirit, each one of us is established in his own, unique personal way towards God, through this most intimate, interior and self-effacing presence of the Lord the Comforter, at the very heart of our being. And this most mysterious and inward aspect of the Church's faith is signified and made plain in a special way by those who are called to live their solidarity with their fellow-men in silence and solitude. There is need here for a very deliberate reciprocity between those who follow this way and those who are called to the sacramental hierarchy of the Church, itself also a gift of the Holy Spirit. The life of one who lives in great isolation, cut off for long periods from any outward participation in the sacramental life of the Church, is likely to appear a scandal to those who have failed to measure the true nature of the diversity of callings within the Body. But at the same time, and more profoundly, it may be seen as a witness to the constant presence and power of the Holy Spirit, who is 'everywhere present and filling all things'; and as a rebuke to the Church's temptation to submit the freedom of her members 'to a kind of sacramental determinism', while itself constituting a kind of sacramental representation of the freedom which the Spirit gives to each one of us to grow up into our adoption in Christ, sons in the Son, children of the one Father.

CONCLUSION

I have spoken about the solitary life in relation to the life of the Church and of all mankind, and I hope to have suggested reasons why the vocation of the one who is summoned to live in physical solitude is of the utmost importance to all his fellow-men in helping them to understand and discover that dimension of solitude which lies at the heart of every life. About the solitary life in itself I have not ventured to speak, being in no way qualified to do so. I should prefer to conclude with the words of a true hermit — Thomas Merton — which may act as a corrective to any tendency to put too much trust in formulations.

The solitary life is an arid, rugged purification of the heart. St Jerome and St Eucherius have written rhapsodies about the flowering desert, but Jerome was the busiest hermit that ever lived and Eucherius was a bishop who admired the hermit brethren of Lérins only from afar ... The true solitary is not called to an illusion, to the contemplation of himself as a solitary. He is called to the nakedness and hunger of a more primitive and honest condition. The condition of a stranger and a wanderer on the face of the earth, who has been called out of what was familiar to him in order to seek strangely and painfully after he knows not what. [11]

NOTES

1. St Peter Damian, *Selected Writings on the Spiritual Life*, trans. Patricia McNulty (Faber 1959) p. 57.

2. Ibid. pp. 58–9.

3. Ibid. pp. 63–4.

4. For a historical consideration of these questions see D. J. Chitty, *The Desert A City*, 2nd Edn 1977.

5. An English translation of the whole poem may be found in Joseph P. Clancy, *The Earliest Welsh Poetry* (1970) pp. 117–18. See also Gwyn Williams, *An Introduction to Welsh Poetry* (Faber 1953) p. 73. The translation given here is adapted from Gwyn Williams's. (Enlli is the Welsh name for Bardsey.)

6. I am deeply indebted to Sir Idris Foster for help in the exegesis of this poem. On the meaning of *gwrthrych* see D. A. Binchy, *Celtic and Anglo-Saxon Kingship* (Oxford 1970) pp. 27–8.

7. Vladimir Lossky, *In the Image and Likeness of God* (Mowbray 1975) p. 107.

8. Ibid. p. 105.

9. Ibid. p. 108.

10. Ibid. p. 192.

11. Chapter 'The Philosophy of Solitude' in *Disputed Questions* (Hollis & Carter 1961) p. 198.

III

REVELATION AND ART

Creation, Incarnation, Interpretation

The title of this chapter is in itself a Trinitarian one. It speaks of creation, incarnation, and interpretation. And though in every work of the Godhead, all three persons are at one, yet we cannot but think in creation primarily of the Father, in incarnation of the Son, and in interpretation of the Spirit. And all that I can hope to do in these pages is to sketch in certain elements of background to the more particular discussion of the relation of man's artistic activities to the proclamation of the Christian message, to the revelation of the Father, the Son, and the Holy Spirit.

And in these words the whole nature of the Christian message, and of our human life is indicated. All comes from God, and ends in him. And man is made in the image of the triune Godhead, made in order that he may share in the eternal life and love of the three persons. And it is this same God who is at work both in creation and redemption. In both stages of God's revelation of his love and glory, the Son and the Holy Spirit are the two hands of love, shaping the creation, renewing the creation after the pattern of the divine nature.

In saying this we guard ourselves both from the mistake of starting from man, from human creativity, and also from the mistake of narrowing down the acts of God to a purely religious sphere. We must avoid the liberal tendency which would think of God simply as the final term of man's evolution and development. We must avoid the neo-orthodox tendency which, by denying the real correlation between divine and human, would restrict the acts of God to a purely Biblical realm, and would thereby regard artistic activity as somehow almost irrelevant to God's revelation of himself. We must recognise that the coming of Christ is not only a judgement upon man's activity and thought, but also its recapitulation and fulfilment. In him, our human nature, wonderfully created in the beginning is still more wonderfully renewed, so that by his partaking of our human nature, we may be made partakers of his divine nature.

In this chapter, I shall try first of all to say something about God's work in creation, and about man's capacity for creation, 'making' poetry as part of the image of God in man. Here I shall attempt to speak of man's artistic activities, in singing, painting, building, and carving in their widest and most general forms.

Then I shall come to speak of incarnation and redemption, and of man's artistic activities as they are used within that sphere, to represent the reality both of God's showing of himself to us, and of man's response of faith and adoration. Here I shall be speaking of liturgical art, painting and music, singing and writing and building as used within the body of Christ.

Finally I shall try to say a little about the work of the Spirit of God as interpreter, and translator, considering the work of the comforter as the one who establishes communication between man and man, between man and God.

'God saw all that he had made, and behold it was very good.' There is I suppose no more dreadful sign of the impoverishment of our Western Christianity than the way in which this thought has faded from the minds of Christian people. The thought of God has been restricted to the world of man, to the world of ideas, to the world of religion. And finally in practice, we tend to treat God as if he were no more than a concept which we are pleased to entertain.

In a rather notable outburst in his book *Spiritus Creator*, Professor Regin Prenter exclaims, 'The fact that the thought of the creation in Luther is always trinitarian, so that the preservation and upholding of the whole creation can be attributed to the Holy Spirit ... may perhaps appear curious to a post-pietist theology which is accustomed to confine talk of the Holy Spirit to the realm of religious life and which therefore attempts to push these thoughts in Luther to one side as something inessential. But they are to be found constantly in his writings and at the most different periods of his life, when he has occasion to expound the creation narrative.

'But it should cause us no special surprise, that such thoughts about the Holy Spirit's cosmic work are to be found in Luther. For these are Biblical thoughts which he takes up. "When thou hidest thy face they are troubled: when thou takest away their breath (spirit) they die, and are turned again to their dust. When thou lettest thy breath go forth they shall be made, and thou shalt renew the face of the earth. The glorious majesty of the Lord shall endure for ever. The Lord shall rejoice in his works." The Bible – and Luther who lived in a Biblical world picture – knows of no world which has an existence independently of the triune God. For Biblical, and for Lutheran, Christianity, the fact that we live and breathe – bodily – that we break bread and drink wine which gladdens man's heart, and use His gifts for our rejoicing, is as much a work of God's spirit, the same spirit which gives us new birth in baptism and strengthens us in temptation, as is the fact that we repent and go to Church. We, on the other hand, live with a world picture, in which nature is understood as a machine which goes by itself, and man is a sovereign lord who only needs God when he comes to die, or possibly to repent.' [1]

Within this created order in which God has placed him, man rejoices not only in eating and drinking, though he does that, and those acts, the primary social acts of man have certainly their own divine reference, but also in certain other activities which we are accustomed to call artistic, the arts. Man sings, he composes verse, he paints, he carves. Here too, he is rejoicing in God's works. And he seems in some strange way to be participating, at his own level, in the divine activity itself. For God who is himself creator, has planted in man this desire and capacity to create. And if all human activity has a symbolic character, that is to say, points beyond itself to some further reality, then artistic activity of whatever sort is particularly charged with this mysterious, symbolic quality. It is very evidently not self explanatory. It contains and reveals meanings and purposes which are not apparent on the surface.

It is indeed difficult to speak with precision on so vast a subject. But this intuition, that in our experience of music or painting or poetry we are in some way in touch with eternal realities, is I suppose so universal as to be undeniable. The novelist or playwright reveals to us the depths and seriousness of the human situation, the poet reveals the nature of this world as it really is; the musician gives us a vision of an order and a beauty which seem untouched by time. And all this is done by means of material things, symbolic objects and words, and ordered sequence of sounds.

I should like to quote at this point from one of the earlier novels of Iris Murdoch. In *The Bell*, the heroine, Dora, has reached something of a crisis of depression. She goes almost unintentionally into the National Gallery, where she had often been before. 'Dora was always moved by the pictures. To-day she was moved but in a new way. She marvelled, with a kind of gratitude, that they were all still there, and her heart was filled with love for the pictures, their authority, their marvellous generosity, their splendour. It occurred to her that here at last was something real and something perfect . . . Here was something which her consciousness could not wretchedly devour, and by making it part of her fantasy, make it worthless . . . The pictures were something real, outside herself, which spoke to her kindly yet in sovereign tones, something superior and good whose presence destroyed the dreamy trance-like solipsism of her earlier mood. When the world had seemed to be subjective it had seemed to be without interest and value. But now there was something else in it after all.

'These thoughts, not clearly articulated, flitted through Dora's mind. She had never thought about the pictures in this way before; nor did she draw now any very explicit moral. Yet she felt that she had had a revelation. She looked at the radiant, sombre, tender, powerful canvas of Gainsborough and felt a sudden desire to go down on her knees before it, embracing it, shedding tears.' [2]

It is unnecessary to underline the nature of the experience so movingly described here. But it may be proper to add that for many of our contemporaries, very many, this sort of revelatory experience before some work of art, be it music or painting, is perhaps, the nearest that they come to the explicit knowledge of the divine. Into this is poured all the longing and adoration and gratitude which should be offered directly to God in praise and worship. And I think in my own life of long evenings as a schoolboy spent in the company of thousands of other young people in the Promenade

Concerts in London; and for many in the audience, this was their only explicit contact with a world beyond that of time.

Of course this general revelatory character of art is, you will say, a very uncertain and confused thing. And this is certainly true. The world is fallen. Man has misused the capacities which God has planted in him. His artistic activities may take on a demonic rather than a divine character. But this does not destroy the fact that the world and man are still in their essence, good. And that evil is a disfigurement, a distortion of some good thing which still remains. Nor, I think, do we truly exalt God's work in redemption, by an attempt to vilify and degrade the remaining elements of beauty and goodness in the created order. The work of the Word and the Spirit in the Church is not as poor a thing that it will suffer by comparison with the greatest goodness that manifests itself in the world and in human life. We need not be afraid to acknowledge the activity of God in creation, nor even the dignity of fallen man. For in the incarnation of the Word we have still more. As one of our seventeenth-century bishops, Edward Reynolds, writes: 'The sum and total of all God's works are the world and the Church; the world is called *kosmos*, for the beauty and comeliness of it, in which, everything was very good when the Lord took a view of it. But the Lord hath chosen His Church, upon which to bestow more abundant glory. It is called a land of ornament (Dan. 11:16), a land of desire (Jer. 3:1), in the building whereof the Lord is said to appear in His glory (Ps. 102:16). The world is beautified with the power and wisdom of God, the Church, besides that, with His love and grace. In the world we have the footprints of His greatness, but in the Church we have the image of His holiness. The World was made by him, the Church like him, the World to show forth His glory, the Church to enjoy it, the World a tenement for His creatures to dwell in, the Church a palace for himself to dwell in. He hath desired it for His habitation; it is His rest for ever.' [3] Here in the Church which is the body of Christ, the communion of the Holy Spirit, we have God's new presence among men, his inhabitation, his incarnation.

Here we embark on a new stage in our development of this subject, the incarnation of the Word of God. If the activities of man,

made in God's image, have all some reference to God, here in
the union of God with man in the person of the incarnate Lord, that
reference becomes immediate and explicit. In Christ, artistic activity
takes on a new significance. The symbolic character of all artistic
work receives its full expression, its true foundation in the fact that
God reveals himself in particular events, in taking flesh, and in the
sacraments of the Word made flesh.

We come here to liturgical art, to the use of man's creative power
in the direct service of the confession of God's glory and goodness
in the worship of the Church. And here we have to face at once the
challenge of the Cross. Is it possible in face of this reality to maintain that man's creative powers can be used to God's glory? In face
of this revelation of the force of evil in man and in the world, is it
still possible to speak of the goodness of all things that God has
made? In our English-speaking Christianity, at least, we know a
powerful tradition which denies the use of music, poetry, symbolism
and colour in the worship of God; and which if it has not been able
to remove the elements of bread and wine from the supper of the
Lord, and water from the act of baptism, has yet in general denied
any presence of God in this material world.

While I feel strongly that we must reject the conclusions of this
Puritan tradition, yet I am equally convinced that we must take its
protest seriously, and receive the element of truth which it contains.
There must be in all liturgical or sacred art an element of renunciation, of purification, of stripping. We recognise intuitively a
necessity for a certain severity and restraint, in liturgical music, in
church architecture, in iconography. And if there comes again in
Christian art a moment of exuberance, and sheer joy, it is a moment
which is arrived at through this process of purification.

It is not accidental that many of the greatest achievements of
liturgical art, in music for instance, the plainsong of the Western
Church, in iconography the development of that art in late Byzantine and medieval Russia, in architecture, the buildings of the
romanesque and early Gothic periods, should all have taken place
within, or in close contact with, monastic communities. It is only in
that context of a radical asceticism that a truly Christian art can
flourish. For if the material world is to be used as a direct expression
of the divine glory, it can only be done through the transfiguration

of man's mind and will and flesh by the grace of God, by the power of the Holy Spirit. And this involves a radical repentance, a renewing of man's mind so that it may be conformed to the will of God. This demands at the outset a recognition of the inadequacy of words to describe the fullness of the divine glory, the inability of our words to express the fullness of God's word, so that all our preaching and our worship must be set within a context of silence or, rather, must tend toward silence. Here again the monastery is of the greatest significance, for it is only in the setting of a life in which the gift of speech is used primarily, in some cases almost exclusively, in order to speak to God, that we can discover the full meaning of the words of the liturgy. The same words of the psalms, for instance, coming from a monastic choir, gain a new significance on account of the silence from which they proceed.

This recognition of a certain primacy of silence, if I may so call it, does not prevent the use of painting and music in the life of the Church, any more than it inhibits the use of words either in worship or theology. What it does is to prevent us from falling into the fatal error so common both in Catholicism and Protestantism, of thinking that we have comprehended and can express the fullness of God's revelation either in a closed system of human concepts, or in purely human and worldly artistic techniques. I would suggest that this is perhaps the significance of the reversal of perspective in Byzantine icons. The icon is not meant, any more than the writing of the theologian, to introduce you into a self-sufficient, self-contained, human world. It is meant rather to open your eyes to the infinite possibilities of the mystery of God. It is a window into eternity. Like the monastic community, like the whole Church, the work of an artist or theologian becomes an eschatological sign, a sign of the presence in this age, of the indescribable glory of the age to come.

It is this which creates the impassable gulf between true iconography and religious painting, and which to my mind makes it very difficult for a purely naturalistic depiction of the human body to be satisfactory in a liturgical context. In iconography the painter has made himself the servant of God, has rooted himself in the tradition of the Church, has subjected his ideas to the divine revelation. In religious painting, however religious the subject may be, the artist has simply expressed his own feelings, used the material at his disposal for self-expression. And however legitimate this type of self-expression may be in ordinary artistic creation, it can have no place within the worship of the Church. It is reported of Bernadette of Lourdes that 'shown an album of pictures of our Lady, she rejected with horror the renaissance ones: she tolerated Fra Angelico's; but lingered with a certain satisfaction over quite early, rigid, depersonalized mosaics or frescoes.'[4] And how true her instinct was, in rejecting the religious paintings of the Renaissance, whatever their aesthetic merit, as valueless from the strictly spiritual point of view. The iconographer, like the priest at the altar, has to offer his whole being to the service of God, but no more than the priest should he obtrude his own personality, or use his activity as a means of self-expression.

The greatest source of our confusion here is the commonly received belief that the Christian tradition of asceticism, involves the type of rejection of the material world which we find in Puritanism. But the truth is quite otherwise. For while the Puritan denied the flesh, because he believed it had little or no connection with the divine, the monk denies it for totally different reasons. It is difficult to escape the conclusion that in Puritanism one has simply an almost blind preference for intellectual, abstract images, instead of visual ones. The communication of the gospel must be done solely at the conscious level of thought. So that while it is absolutely right to describe the crucifixion with every verbal means available, in the sermon and in the hymns, it is absolutely unthinkable, in that tradition, to use a crucifix. And an Englishman visiting Scandinavia must feel that the retention of images in the churches has a deeper significance for Lutheran Christianity than many of us have yet realised.[5] But while the Puritan renounces *some* forms of human activity as inappropriate to the service of God, the monk renounces all in order that all, the *whole* man, spirit, mind and body, may be transfigured by the divine glory and that God's glory may shine out not only in men's characters and wills, but in their very bodies. And we may ask, how does this link up with our understanding of the Pauline dualism of flesh and spirit, where flesh does *not* mean physical nature as opposed to intellectual, and spirit does *not* mean immaterial, but where both terms can refer to the whole man turned towards or away from God?

It would be impossible in these pages to develop this theme at length, but it seems to me of such surpassing importance, particularly for an understanding of Eastern iconography, that I must pause over it for a moment.

God became man, in order that by God's grace man might become God. That is the very heart of the gospel as it is understood by the Fathers of the Church. In the incarnation, God took flesh, so that through material things the divine glory might be revealed. 'That which was from the beginning, which we have heard, which we have seen with our eyes, which we have looked upon, and our hands have handled, the Word of Life.' The body which in the resurrection is to share in eternal life, even in this world has its share in the life of God. This is the great mystery, the great sacrament upon which all the other mysteries, sacraments of the Christian life, depend. To quote Edward Reynolds again, 'It were almost a contradiction in anything, save God's mercy, to be so deep as that no thought can fathom it, and yet so obvious that each eye can see it.' "*Handle me and see*; for a spiritual substance hath not flesh' — was sometimes the argument of Christ; and yet '*Handle and see, take and eat*, for a spiritual grace is conveyed in flesh' is the sacrament of Christ. So humble is his mercy, that, since we cannot raise our understandings to the comprehension of divine mysteries, he will bring down and submit those mysteries to the apprehension of our senses.[6]

And surely the Orthodox Church is right when it sees the incarnation of the Word, not as an isolated, single event, but as a revelation of God's love which wills to redeem and transfigure the whole created universe. The person of Jesus of Nazareth in whom all the fullness of the godhead dwells is to be the focal point from which the divine presence is to radiate out into the world, and bring the Church into being. The presence of God is to be found throughout the life of the Church. 'The world (he has made) a tenement for his creatures to dwell in; the Church a palace for himself to dwell in.'

It is on this understanding of the incarnation, and of the inhabitation of Christ in the Church by the Spirit, that the Orthodox doctrine of icons, and the practice of the veneration of icons is founded. St John of Damascus writes in his classical treatise *In Defence of the Holy Icons*: 'Of old, God the incorporeal and uncircumscribed was not depicted at all. But now that God has appeared in the flesh and lived among men, I make an image of the God who can be seen. I do not venerate matter, but I venerate the Creator of matter, who for my sake became material and designed to dwell in matter, who through matter effected my salvation ... matter, filled with divine power and grace, was the means through which came my salvation.'[7]

And it seems to me, at least, profoundly right that in the Orthodox Church, not only the consecrated elements in the holy eucharist, but also the altar, the book of the gospels, the holy icons, the relics of the saints, and the persons of the priests and people, should all be treated with reverence as holy things. For all are in different ways and different degrees symbols of Christ, and in all God makes his presence known.

It is this belief which must make for the Orthodox the veneration of icons not only a matter of practice, but at least in some way or other, a matter of principle. 'In the eyes of the Church', writes Leonid Ouspensky, 'the denial of the icon of Christ appears as a denial of the truth and immutability of the fact of his becoming man, and therefore of the whole divine dispensation. Defending the icon in the period of iconoclasm, the Church was not defending merely its educational role and, still less, its aesthetic value; it was fighting for the very foundations of the Christian faith, the visible testimony of God become man as the basis of our salvation.'[8] It is not easy to see how this applies in our Western situation, where the theologically uncontrolled and undisciplined use of images in the Middle Ages led to the inevitable, and in many respects, justified reaction of the Reformers. It may be best for us at present to use great restraint in the use of imagery on the Church. But we need to recognise the way in which for the Orthodox the doctrine of the Incarnation is bound up indissolubly with the cultus of the Mother of God and the Saints, and the veneration of the icons.

Here is one of the factors which gives to Orthodoxy its character of triumph and rejoicing. Even here and now the world is being restored to its original glory. 'For the Russians the artistic perfection of the icon was not only a reflection of the celestial glory – it was a concrete example of matter restored to its original harmony and beauty, and serving as a vehicle of the Spirit. The icons were part of the transfigured cosmos.' [9] St John of Damascus declares, 'The icon is a song of triumph and a revelation, and an enduring monument,' it is a sign of the triumph of God's grace over the dark elements in matter and in man's heart, and the restoration of the true order of creation.

This teaching on the transfiguration of the world through Christ, and the participation of the body in the life of grace, receives perhaps its fullest form in the writings of St Gregory Palamas. The fourteenth-century controversies in which he took part turned on just these things, the nature of the transfiguration, and the place of the body in prayer. And this strictly monastic author can write in such terms as these, 'that spiritual joy which comes from the spirit into the body is not corrupted by its communion with the body, but rather transforms the body and makes it spiritual . . . so that the whole man becomes spirit, as it is written, "That which is born of the Spirit is Spirit" or again "The soul is not alone in receiving a foretaste of the good things which are yet to come; the body receives them also, which to this end follows the way of the gospel, together with the soul." ' [10] It was no accident that the highest point of Byzantine icon painting should have been reached at just this moment when Palamas was writing, icon painting which blends the divine with the human in a miraculous manner, and which proceeds, 'not by conversion of the Godhead into flesh, but by taking of the manhood into God'.

That this teaching about man's body was not unknown in the West during the middle ages could be shown by quoting the writings of at least some of the early Cistercians. But it is painfully evident that it has almost disappeared from the Christian consciousness, both in Catholicism and Protestantism, since the time of the Reformation, and the seventeenth century. Too often it has been assumed that the material is simply irrelevant to the divine life, that spiritual equals immaterial, that religion is concerned only with man's mind and will and soul, which have somehow been considered as existing without any connection with man's body, and the world in which it lives. In general it would seem that the great sacramental and symbolic principle that it is in and through material things that the divine glory is revealed, has been lost to sight, so that the light of God has been seen not as transfiguring the world which he has made, but as a shadow which darkens the earth. It has remained for those outside the Church, who have yet received some vision of the divine, to speak of this as it should be spoken of. Rilke, in a passage where ironically enough he thinks of himself as opposing Christian doctrine, writes, 'Nature, the things we associate with and use, are provisional and perishable; but so long as we are here, they are our possessions and our friendship; sharers in our trouble and gladness, just as they have been the confidants of our ancestors. Therefore, not only must all that is here not be vilified or degraded, but, just because of that very provisionality they share with us, all these appearances and things should be, in the most fervent sense, comprehended by us and transformed. Transformed? Yes, for our task is to stamp this provisional, perishing earth into ourselves, so deeply, so painfully and passionately, that its being may rise again "invisibly" in us. We are the bees of the invisible. *Nous butinons éperdument le miel du visible, pour l'accumaler dans la grande ruche d'or de l'Invisible.*' [11] The poet does not speak with theological accuracy; but surely what he is saying corresponds more truly to the nature of God's revelation and man's response as we find it in the Bible and in the Fathers than does much of the anaemic, immaterial piety of both Catholicism and Protestantism. Still more ironical and sad, are those passages in which the older Wordsworth, in the interest of what he believed theological accuracy, altered the somewhat pantheistic expressions of his youth, and thereby deprived his writings not only of something of poetic life, but also of much of their genuinely theological quality.

So far we have spoken of God's act in creation, of God's act in incarnation and redemption, both of them terrifying mysteries which entirely surpass our means of expression. And now we must turn to the third stage of God's dispensation, to the work of the Holy Spirit in the Church, and in the hearts of men. For if, as we noted at the beginning, both the Word and the Spirit are active in creation, yet the incarnation of the Word at Bethlehem, and the descent of the Spirit on the Church at Pentecost inaugurate a new and more wonderful presence of God amongst men. Here when we try to speak of the Holy Spirit, this most intimate and hidden mystery, our language becomes still more faltering and inadequate. Vladimir

Lossky, in his *Mystical Theology of the Eastern Church*, says, 'We confess the Deity of the Holy Spirit in common with that of the Father and that of the Son; we confess the Holy Trinity. But the Person of the Holy Spirit Himself who reveals these truths to us, and who renders them inwardly luminous, manifest, almost tangible to us, nevertheless remains Himself undisclosed and hidden, concealed by the deity which He reveals to us, by the gift which he imparts.'[12] And in another place he speaks of the way in which 'when the thought of the Fathers ... touches on this mysterious reality, it renounces the dogmatic expressions which are customary ... the key changes, and the Fathers begin to speak another language, as if their whole being responded to the contact with the most intimate, the most personal mystery which filled them with a limitless wonder, a sort of intoxication.'[13]

This sense of wonder at the overflowing generosity of the divine nature is to be found for instance in a famous passage of St Basil's work on the Holy Spirit, 'Who, as he writes, ungrudgingly imparts his own excellence ... for whom all things living long according to their excellence, being as it were refreshed by his breath, and assisted to attain their own proper and natural end; perfective of all else, himself lacking nothing, who lives not because He is endowed with life but because he is the giver of life; ... [he is] the source of sanctification, the light of the mind, who illuminates every faculty of reason in its search for truth; unapproachable by nature but accessible on account of his goodness; wholly present everywhere, and wholly present with each individual . . . .'[14] The Holy Spirit seems as it were to burst the bounds of the divine nature in the outpouring of God's glory in his work of creation. Here surely is some glimpse of the meaning of the word blessing, God's goodness over all his works. Here too is the God-given element in the whole development of modern science. 'Astronomers, naturalists, geologists, physicists, and psychologists, are fascinated by the excellence, the splendour and the mystery of the universe they observe. Their impulse to observe does not unfortunately come from their Christian faith, for often they have none. But they have retained their God-given desire to know, and their capacity to wonder and admire. Clearly the creator must be whatever else He is – exuberant, lively, lavish, ingenious and ecstatically gay.'[15] At this point too, surely, the insight of the artist and the investigation of the scientist meet in a common amazement before the mystery of the created world; an amazement which is how much greater when we turn from the world to its creator. None the less, the terms which I am given, speaking of interpretation, indicate that in speaking of the Spirit, we are to think less of his work in creation than of the illumination of the mind in its search for truth, and of that Catholic work by which he creates the unity of all.

The Holy Spirit, the God *within* us, is also above all the God *between* us, the love which unites men with one another and with God. Here we come to the Spirit's great work of enlightenment and translation. He takes the things of Christ and shows them to us. So that the events of the gospel become real and accessible for every time and every nation; he relates us to God and in doing so, relates us to one another. Thus we discover that unity in diversity, that common life, in which 'that which belongs to all belongs to each, and that which is particular to some belongs to all in the unity of faith and love',[16] which is the root meaning of the word Catholic. It is not by the suppression of each unique person that the Holy Spirit creates the Catholic unity. Rather it is in the common life of all that each one finds his own fulfilment. And it is the one Spirit who creates the relationships, interpreting from one to another, and who fulfils each particular one, giving different gifts to each.

When we consider the amount of misunderstanding which exists in the world, between individuals, between groups, between nations, owing to a failure to hear and listen to one another's words, we begin to see the meaning of this work of the Spirit, as interpreter, as peacemaker, restoring the broken relationships between men and nations. And when we consider how much artistic activity is rendered fruitless and sterile by a failure to communicate and how often the shock of recognition which the Spirit brings about fails to take place, we see again in this particular sphere how necessary this work of the Spirit is. Here it seems to me that the artist within the Church has a particular gift and opportunity. For he has at least the elements of a common language with his fellow Christians, and is sometimes able to make contacts across usually insurmountable barriers. I think in this connection of the way in which plays like *Murder in the Cathedral* can become a living experience when produced in very or-

dinary parishes; or of how questions of church architecture and symbolism become real when there is a parish council which is willing to
shoulder its responsibilities in the building of a new church, and an
architect who is a sufficiently mature Christian to see that such a
work must be a co-operative effort in which the congregation must
have as active a share as himself.

These are only small examples of the way in which in the Spirit,
in the Church, the artist is sometimes able to break through that wall
of privacy and individualism which in Western Europe seems to
stultify so much of his activity. And this break-through is important
not only for the artist, but also for the Church. For in face both of
the non-European cultures of Asia and Africa and of the de-
christianised masses of Western Europe, the Church too knows this
failure to communicate. Here again the work of the artist, the work
of the Spirit as interpreter is of vital importance. One cannot dictate
how this will happen. The Spirit who is free, and the giver of life,
must and will create new forms of expression, breaking through the
often formalised structures of our conventional church life. As a multiplicity of new forms springs up, so it will become more clear that
Christianity is not merely a Western European phenomenon, but is
the fulfilment and the judgement of all human culture. And surely
this must lead to a deeper understanding of the meaning of the word
Catholic, an understanding of its depth and quality, as well as of its
breadth and extension.

At the beginning of this chapter, we considered the way in which
in all the acts of God, Father, Son and Holy Spirit work together;
and now having traced the activity of the Father in creation, of the
Son in redemption, we have spoken however inadequately of the
work of the Spirit in interpretation. And this has brought us inevitably to the thought not only of the Spirit's work as revealed in
artistic interpretation, but of the Spirit's work in opening the hearts
and minds of Christ's people to one another, and thereby creating
Christian unity. 'When thou hidest thy face, they are troubled;
when thou takest away their breath, they die . . . when thou lettest
thy breath go forth, they shall be made, and thou shalt renew the
face of the earth.' And at this time of a universal stirring within
Christendom, when all the old barriers are coming down, there
would seem to arise toward God from all our separated churches a

fervent epiclesis, a calling upon the Holy Spirit who alone can bring new life and unity to the valley of dry bones in which we find ourselves. *Veni, Sancte Spiritus, reple tuorum corda fidelium, Et tui amoris in eis ignem accende, qui per diversitatem linguarum cunctarum gentes in unitate fidei congregasti. Emitte Spiritum tuum, Domine et creabuntur, et renovabis faciem terrae.* Come Holy Ghost, and fill the hearts of thy faithful people, and kindle in them the fire of thy love, who in the diversity of tongues hast gathered together the nations into the unity of faith. Send out thy Spirit, O Lord, and they shall be made, and thou shalt renew the face of the earth.

NOTES

1. Regin Prenter, *Spiritus Creator*, 2nd ed. pp. 200–1.
2. Iris Murdoch, *The Bell* pp. 191–2.
3. P. E. More and F. L. Cross (edd.), *Anglicanism* p. 771.
4. L. Ouspensky and V. Lossky, *The Meaning of Icons*, p. 44.
5. It is interesting to compare, in this connection, the Puritan rejection of music, with the Scandinavian use of it, and especially with the retention and adaptation of much of the pre-Reformation chant of the Church.
6. More and Cross, op. cit. p. 410.
7. S. John of Damascus, P.G. 94, col. 1245.
8. Ouspensky and Lossky, op. cit. p. 35.
9. N. Zernov, *The Russians and Their Church* p. 108.
10. Quoted in J. Meyendorff, *Introduction à l'Etude de Gregoire Palamas*, pp. 207–8. (E.T. *A Study of Gregory Palamas* pp. 144–5.)
11. R. M. Rilke, *Sonnets to Orpheus* (Eng. translation and introduction by J. P. Leishmann) pp. 18–19.
12. V. Lossky, *The Mystical Theology of the Eastern Church* p. 162.
13. Quoted from a lecture of Lossky's in *Messager de l'Exarchat du Patriarche Russe en Europe Occidentale*, Nos. 30–1. p. 175.
14. St Basil, P.G. 32, col. 108.
15. From a lecture by F. H. Maycock in *How to Conduct Retreats* (ed. Robin Anstey) p. 58.
16. St Peter Damian, P.L. 145, col. 239.

9

The Writer and Tradition

a common theme in Henry Vaughan and Thomas Merton

One of Wales's best-loved poets of this present century, Waldo Williams, in a poem called 'What is man?' asks the question 'What is love of country?'

Beth yw gwladgarwch?
and gives the reply
    Cadw ty
    Mewn cwmwl tystion.[1]

'Keeping house amidst a cloud of witnesses.' The answer is one which would apply to our love for the Church, the universal family into which we are brought through faith and baptism, no less than it would to that particular family of the nation to which we belong by birth and upbringing. In both cases, truly to love that people means to do all kinds of small, daily, routine things, 'the little things' of which it is said St David spoke on his death bed, in the awareness that we do them in the context of a long tradition, surrounded by many witnesses, from the distant past no less than from our own times.

In thinking of Henry Vaughan, I would want to think of him in this way, as one who in his own century 'kept house' in the valley of the Usk, but always with the knowledge of the cloud of witnesses around him, that cloud in which he himself is now to be numbered. I would think of him therefore not primarily as an outstanding poet — there are others who have done that and can do it with far greater

knowledge than myself — but rather as an authoritative witness to
the wholeness and integrity of the Christian tradition, theological,
sacramental and ecclesial, as well as personal, the tradition by which
he lived, and who speaks for that tradition with the authority which
comes alike from learning and experience.

It is natural enough that the great majority of those who have
written about Vaughan, studying him as a poet, should have
stressed all that is most personal and idiosyncratic in his writing.
That it has its own unique tone and quality no one could deny. But
this fact should not blind us to the possibility of another way of approach, a way which would show us Vaughan standing beside
George Herbert as a representative spokesman of the theological
and spiritual tradition of seventeenth-century Anglicanism. One has
only to compare the theology of the incarnation lying behind a
poem like 'The Knot', with the exposition of the theme of Mary's
place in the mystery of man's redemption to be found in the sermons
of Lancelot Andrewes, to see how firmly Vaughan's position is
rooted in the theology of his Church. [2] To say this is not to deny his
deep interest in hermetic philosophy, nor the influence of his reading
in the hermetic books which is evident in his use of imagery. But as
R. A. Durr wisely remarks, 'Vaughan was entirely capable of absorb-
ing elements of the amorphous hermeticism of his time into his fundamentally Christian belief without feeling heretical . . . just as it is
possible for a man today to incorporate aspects of Freudian or
Jungian psychology or existential philosophy into a fundamentally
Christian view of life.' [3]

Again, in thinking of Vaughan as a spokesman for the wholeness
of the Christian tradition, we must not overlook the fact that he did
not escape the strong currents of conflict and polemic which marked
the age in which he lived. He certainly does much less than justice to
the positive intentions and aspirations of his Puritan adversaries. He
prayed to be able to forgive his enemies, but he did not find it easy.
Nonetheless one of the things which is striking about his work is
the extent to which it goes beyond the divisions which he knew, appealing to the testimony of the undivided Church across the schisms
of the Reformation, across the centuries of the division between
Christian East and West. There is a great longing for unity in him, a
prayer that all may come together in the truth of God.

> Give to thy spouse her perfect and pure dress,
>   Beauty and holiness,
> And so repair these rents, that men may see
>   And say, 'Where God is, all agree.' [4]

It is particularly when we come to consider that neglected part of
Vaughan's work, his prose writings, that we begin to see how important this longing for unity is. By his translations from the Latin,
Vaughan plays his part in that hidden ecumenical movement which
has never altogether ceased at the level of prayer and spirituality.
Despite the gulf at that time existing between Rome and Canterbury, he does not hesitate to take texts from contemporary Jesuit
editions, nor to translate from medieval writers as well as from the
fathers of the early Church. Quietly but certainly he is affirming a
unity across the divisions, looking to that larger communion of the
whole Church 'Eastern, Western and our own', for which Lancelot
Andrewes prayed, and which the seventeenth-century Anglicans
never altogether lost to sight.

My own attention was first drawn to this aspect of Vaughan's
work by the deep interest in him shown by one of the outstanding
exponents of the tradition of Christian spirituality of our own day,
Thomas Merton. As a Cistercian and a monk, no less than as a poet
and a man of letters, Merton felt that it was of vital importance for
him to become familiar with the whole tradition of spirituality
which has come down to us in the English language, in its many
varied strands. He loved the mystics of the fourteenth century and
the recusant writers of the seventeenth, but he was also fully aware
of the distinctive witness of the seventeenth-century Anglicans. He
felt that it was important for Roman Catholics, as they moved into
a much greater use of the vernacular, 'to have some sense of the
Anglican tradition', though he was not over optimistic about the
possibility of this happening on a wide scale. [5]

For himself, this was more than a matter of theoretical interest.
He made use of the *Preces Privatae* of Lancelot Andrewes in his own
night prayer in the hermitage. His love for Traherne is clearly expressed in one of the essays in *Mystics and Zen Masters*. He
welcomed such opportunities as came to him for direct contact with
representatives of the Anglican tradition. What he writes in a

notable passage in *Conjectures of a Guilty Bystander* about desiring to unite in himself 'the thought and devotion of Eastern and Western Christendom, the Greek and the Latin Fathers, the Russian with the Spanish mystics',[6] and thus preparing in himself the reunion of divided Christians, was every bit as true of his attitude towards the separated strands, Anglican, Puritan, Roman Catholic, of the English-speaking tradition which he had inherited.

Of Henry Vaughan in particular he wrote, in a letter of October, 1963, 'Vaughan I have – one of my favourites', and then he adds the perhaps unexpected remark, 'I once thought of bringing out an edition of his translation of Eucherius *De Contemptu Mundi* – but that would be complicated.' [7] That there would have been complications for a twentieth-century Cistercian monk, living in Kentucky rather far from University libraries, in bringing out an edition of a translation made by a Welsh doctor of the seventeenth century, of a fifth-century Latin work in praise of the monastic life, we may well believe. All the same we may regret that it was never done, since it would have been fascinating to read Merton's observations both on the original and the translation, and to have known exactly what it was in Eucherius and in Vaughan's concern with him, which had caught his attention. The very fact that he considered the project is itself a witness to inner continuities of tradition and experience running across very obvious discontinuities of place and history.

Merton was, of course, aware that in coming into contact with Vaughan, he was touching something Welsh as well as something English. It is striking how much the discovery of the Welsh element in his ancestry came to mean to him in the latter years of his life. He speaks about this already in a passage in *Conjectures of a Guilty Bystander*, which seems to date from 1962. In connection with a visit from his Aunt Kit from New Zealand, he writes, 'My grandmother, Gertrude Grierson . . . is one of the people of whom I retain the strongest impressions in my childhood. She taught me the Lord's Prayer. She was born in Wales of a Scotch father. But the best that is in us seems to me to come from her Welsh mother, whose family name was Bird. This is where our faces come from, the face Father had, that I have, that Aunt Kit has; the look, the grin, the brow. It is the Welsh in me that counts; that is what does the strange things, and writes the books, and drives me into the woods. Thank God for the Welsh in me, for all those Birds, those Celts . . . for the Bird face, and the humour, and the silences.' [8] In the last two years of his life, this discovery of Wales was proceeding apace. He read a translation of the hymns of Ann Griffiths, and at once felt a kinship with her. In 1967 he wrote to me of the poetry of R. S. Thomas as 'a marvellous discovery'. [9] A little later he made another still greater find, and began to explore the work of David Jones which impressed him enormously. In the last postcard which he sent from India a few weeks before his death, he spoke of his hope that he might be able to return to America by way of England in the following May, and then added, 'Can we do Wales then?'

Something of what this desire to visit Wales meant to him can be seen in the opening passages of the long poem called *The Geography of Lograire*, which was published shortly after his death. There are frequent references to Wales in the Prologue, 'holy, green Wales', and there is the suggestion of a tension of opposites within him, between English and Welsh, plains and hills, marshes and mountains, 'two seas in myself, Irish and German'. [10] The geography of his own inner life, which Merton is exploring in this strange, cryptic work could not be separated from the geography of Britain. This most universal of men, with his love for France where he was born, his delight in the poets of South America, both Spanish and Portuguese, his sense of affinity with the cultures of despised and primitive peoples and his deep understanding of the spiritual traditions of the Far East, yet knew that his roots were here, and that though the greater part of his life had not been lived in these islands, this was where his ancestors came from. He wished to gather up and reconcile within himself not only the separated families of Christendom, but also these elements in his own ancestry, for he knew that in some strange way, each one of us is called to sum up and resume the histories of the peoples from which we come. As has been well said of David Jones, 'by birth a man of divided loyalties, [he became] above all, the poet of reconciliation'. [11]

I do not suggest that all these factors were consciously in Merton's mind when he first felt attracted to Vaughan and to his translation of St Eucherius. There were other and more obvious things to draw the attention of both men to the work of this distinguished

but little-known fifth-century writer. For one thing there was the excellence of his Latin style, highly praised by Erasmus and much admired by the scholars of the seventeenth century. Merton shared this
admiration, considering Eucherius the finest writer of the school of
Lérins. One can see from his translation of the Life of St Paulinus of
Nola that Vaughan no less than Merton had a special love for the
Latin writers of this period in whose work the presence both of the
old classical culture of Rome and of the new impulse of Christian
monasticism is so strongly felt. More than the style however there
was the content of the work in question, Eucherius's exposure of the
vanity of fame and riches. And here one can only regret that
Vaughan never translated, or perhaps could not find a publisher for
Eucherius's companion treatise, *De Laude Eremi*. With its eloquent
praise of the life of solitude and prayer, it gives the positive side to
the somewhat negative argument of *De Contemptu Mundi*. It is
possible that, had the projected edition come to birth, Merton might
have added a translation of this latter work to Vaughan's translation
of the former one. As it is, there is something highly appropriate in
the fact that both men should have been united in their admiration
for one of the outstanding representatives of the monastic school of
Lérins, a school which exercised considerable influence on the early
centuries of Celtic and Anglo-Saxon monasticism.

Merton had indeed a very strong feeling of kinship with the
monastic writers, Greek and Latin, who date from the period of the
collapse of the Roman Empire. Living at a time of rapid change and
disintegration, not altogether unlike our own, they turned from the
world towards God in a movement of radical rejection of worldly
aims and values. Then, in a way, which perhaps was not wholly expected, they found that the world was being given back to them,
that they were called to preserve human values, as well as to bear
their uncompromising witness to the absolute nature of the demands
of God. To find God, they tell us that we must leave all things;
there can be no doubt for them about the necessity of renunciation.
But having found God, we find that in him all things are given back
to us. The world, which in one sense represents human society
closed to God's action, in another sense is seen as his creation, full of
hints and glimpses of his glory. Man himself, when he is known as
the son of an eternal Father, is revealed in the true glory of his

nature. There is here what we may call a monastic or eschatological humanism. It is an attitude which can entertain a delight in humane learning and can cherish what is beautiful, precisely because it knows that these things are not ultimate, not the final cause of man's meaning and man's joy. As Merton remarks of Eucherius's own writing, 'In a sense it celebrates the world which it seems to contemn.'

In our own time, Merton has been a great and creative spokesman for this tradition, perhaps the most influential and widely heard monastic writer in English since the reformation. Vaughan's own way, of course, was different, his influence has never been so extensive. Yet we might remember the very close links between George Herbert, who so greatly influenced him, and the community at Little Gidding, which in the seventeenth-century Church of England incarnated many of the values of the monastic life. Indeed the monastic theme in Vaughan's own life and writing is one which deserves to be further considered. Choosing to live, as he did, on the margin of the society of his own day, he felt a strong attraction to those in the past who had made similar if more radical decisions. In one of the original passages in his life of St Paulinus, he speaks of the choice of the monastic life, as 'a great deed; so great that none nowadays think of doing it. "Go thy way, sell whatsoever thou hast and give to the poor" is a commandment, as well as "Take up the Cross and follow me". This last cannot be done but by doing the first.' [12] In *Man in Darkness* he translates at length and with evident delight from St Jerome's description of his visit to the monks of the Egyptian desert. He too is telling us that those who learn to love God above all things and before all things, find that it becomes possible to love him in all things and through all things as well.

There is a remarkable passage to this effect in Eucherius, where he speaks of the faculty of sight. Left to itself, sight is easily ensnared 'by the deceitful looks of temporal things', but guided by God's grace it can become the means by which we pass to the contemplation of a light beyond the senses and enjoy a felicity not bounded by this world. 'If a sober and virtuous use were made of the eye, we might by that very faculty be drawn to a certain sacred longing after immortality and the powers of the world to come; if

that admiration which by contemplating the rare frame of the world
we are usually filled with, were returned upon the glorious Creator
of it, by our praises and benediction of him, or if we would meditate
what a copious, active and boundless light shall fill our eyes in the
state of immortality, seeing so fair a luminary is allowed us here in
the state of corruption; or what transcendent beauty shall be given
to all things in that eternal world, seeing this transitory one is so full
of majesty and freshness. . . .' [13] Such a movement from the contemplation of the beauties of this world to the beauties of the world
which is to come, is characteristic alike of Merton and of the poet
who could write,

> O Knowing, glorious Spirit, when
> Thou shalt restore trees, beasts and men,
> When thou shalt make all new again,
> Destroying only death and pain,
> Give him amongst thy works a place,
> Who in them loved and sought thy face. [14]

But there is another element in Eucherius which doubtless ap-
pealed in different ways, both to Merton and to Vaughan. It is his
sense of the communion of saints. In the course of his treatise he
calls on a number of eminent witnesses, men of distinction of his
own and the previous century, who had abandoned their positions
in Roman society in order to follow the call of Christ. His work
contains a kind of roll-call of many of the writers whose influence
contributed to the making of seventeenth-century Anglicanism and
whose power has been felt again in our own time in the revival of
patristic studies, in which Merton participated. 'Clement the
Roman, of the stock of the Caesars, and the ancient lineage of the
Senators, a person fraught with science and most skilful in the liberal
arts . . . Gregory of Pontus, a minister of holy things, famous at first
for his humane learning and eloquence . . . Gregory Nazianzen,
another holy Father, given also at first to philosophy and humane
literature, (who) declined at last these worldly rudiments, and embraced the true and heavenly philosophy; to whose industry also we
owe no meaner a person than Basil the Great . . . Paulinus, Bishop
of Nola, the great ornament and light of France . . . Hilarius of late

and Petronius now in Italy, both of them out of the fulness of secular honours and power betook themselves to this course; the one entering into religion, the other into the priesthood. And when shall I have done with this great cloud of witnesses, if I should bring into the field all those eloquent contenders for the faith, Firmilianus, Minutius, Cyprian, Hilary, Chrysostom, Ambrose?' [15] Here commemorated are doctors and fathers, both Greek and Latin, many of them bishops, many of them monks, writers to whose authority Vaughan and his contemporaries turned in their attempt to mark out a middle way between the two parties to the reformation controversy.

In appealing to such authoritative teachers, the Christian writer or scholar, be he poet or theologian, is not indulging in a servile or external imitation of models from the past. Rather he seeks to let their life and example, their teaching and insight come to life afresh within himself. In the fellowship which the gift of God creates across the ages, we share with them in a common history and a common life. We learn to read the Bible and the tradition from within, 'keeping house' with prophets and patriarchs, with fathers and doctors, because members of one family with them. This both Vaughan and Merton were given to do, in their different ways and in their different measure. Through their withdrawal from an immediate involvement with the affairs of the world, they came to realise and see truths which the world is often blind to. In another of the original passages in his life of Paulinus, Vaughan writes, 'The fame of holy men (like the Kingdom of God) is a seed that grows secretly: the dew that feeds these plants comes from him, that sees in secret, but rewards openly. They are those in the poet

> Which silently, and by none seen
>   grow great and green.

While they labour to conceal and obscure themselves, they shine the more. And this (saith Athanasius in the life of Anthony the Great) is the goodness of God, who useth to glorify his servants, though unwilling, that by their examples he may condemn the world, and teach men that holiness is not above the reach of human nature.' [16]

The saints of whom Vaughan speaks in his writings include those who are publicly acknowledged by the Church, and those who are hidden and unknown, those who come to us from the distant past, and those who have lived in our own times. So when he speaks of 'the many blessed patterns of a holy life', which there have been in the British Church, though he at once goes on to refer to George Herbert, 'a most glorious true saint and seer', it is difficult not to suppose that he also had in mind the great figures of the first age of the British Church, those men and women who rivalled the fathers of the Egyptian desert and the first monks of Lérins in their love of prayer and solitude, and who have left their names like icons on the villages and hamlets of the land of Wales. [17] In that country their presence makes itself almost palpably felt. As another outstanding Welsh poet of our own time, Gwenallt, has said,

> There is no frontier between two worlds in the Church;
> The Church militant upon earth is the same
> As the Church triumphant in Heaven,
> And the saints are in this Church which is two in one,
> They come to worship with us, our small congregation,
> The saints, our oldest ancestors,
> Who built Wales on the foundation
> Of the Cradle, the Cross and the Empty Tomb. [18]

In the communion of past with present which the Holy Spirit brings, the barriers of time are over-passed, the first age is renewed. Vaughan's vision goes even further. The patriarchs of the very beginnings of the Old Testament history, Abraham, Isaac and Jacob, are also living witnesses and examples who walk with us.

If in his prose writings Vaughan speaks most of the great acknowledged saints of the past, in his poems he seems more often to have in mind those outwardly unknown ones, who have been very close to him, and whose examples still live before him, leading him on to the thought of immortality. This is the theme of some of his greatest and best-known poems,

> They are all gone into the world of light
> And I alone sit lingering here . . . [19]

It is also the subject of a poem which, though less well known, is
no less interesting from this point of view.

Joy of my life! while left me here
    And still my love
How in thy absence thou dost steer
    Me from above!
    A life will lead
    This truth commends
    With quick or dead
    It never ends.

Stars are of mighty use; the night
    Is dark and long
The road foul, and where one goes right
    Six may go wrong:
    One twinkling ray
    Shot o'er some cloud
    May clear much way
    And guide a crowd.

God's Saints are shining lights: who stays
    Here long must pass
O'er dark hills, swift streams, and steep ways
    As smooth as glass:
    But these all night
    Like candles shed
    Their beam, and light
    Us into bed.

They are (indeed) our Pillar-fires
    Seen as we go,
They are that city's shining spires
    We travel to.
A swordlike gleam
    Kept man for sin,
    First out: this beam
    Will guide him in.[20]

Here we have an element in Vaughan which brings him very close to the Welsh tradition, and to the poet whose work was cited at the beginning of this lecture. Waldo like Vaughan had a love for star-lit nights. In a most moving poem addressed to his friend and fellow-writer, E. Llwyd Williams, he declares,

Llawn o Nef yw llwyn y nos,
Ynddi mae d'awen heno.
Full of heaven is the grove of night,
Tonight your spirit is in it.[21]

And when Vaughan speaks of 'the world of light', a phrase which as E. C. Pettet remarks 'epitomises all Vaughan's visions of heaven',[22] we are led at once to think of the lines from Waldo's poem 'After the Silent Centuries'.

They are one with the light. They are above my head
Where through the expanse, peace gathers. When the
    sky turns to night
Each one is, for my sight, a rent in the veil.[23]

We are surely right to see in this poem, with its praise of the Catholic martyrs of Wales, written by a poet who was Baptist by upbringing and Quaker by adult conviction, a great ecumenical statement, as well as a great national affirmation. How much it would have delighted Merton had he known it, how deeply would he have appreciated its author!

In all the writers we have cited, there is a sense of unity in multiplicity, of a single heavenly and eternal light shining out in a great variety of forms and colours, of the invading presence of God's love which brings men of different times and of different places together into one, and lays bare the roots of all true brotherhood amongst men. Vaughan himself expresses this in memorable terms in another of the original passages of his life of Paulinus. 'Charity is a relic of paradise, and pity is a strong argument that we are all descended from one man; he that carries this rare jewel about with him will everywhere meet with some kindred. He is quickly acquainted with distressed persons, and their first sight warms his blood. I could believe that the word stranger is a notion received from the posterity of Cain, who killed Abel. The Hebrews in their own tribes, called those of the farthest degree brothers; and sure they erred less from the law of pure nature, than the rest of the nations which were left to their own lusts.' [24]

We know that at the end of his life, Henry Vaughan was sorely troubled by strife within his own immediate family circle. We have the legal records of his unhappy relations with his physically handicapped daughter Katharine. A passage such as this, so eloquent and so evidently deeply felt, only highlights the tragedy of these later dissensions. It may perhaps make us wonder whether an excessive or undiscerning kindness could have lain at the root of some of his difficulties. We cannot know. But the inscription on the tombstone, which lies in the churchyard at Llansantffraed, *Servus Inutilis, Peccator Maximus, Hic Jaceo, Gloria Miserere*, assures us that the Henry Vaughan of 1695 is the same man who in the middle years of his life had seen so deeply into the things of God, and had been given such living words in which to express what he had seen. Through all his shortcomings he remains for us a witness to the light. In the work which he has left us we find an expression of that longing for the restoration of man's innocence and for the coming of the Kingdom of Heaven, which is so powerful, that we recognise in him the touch of sanctity and know that the place, where he lived, will remain a holy place in the history of his Church and people.

'What is understanding?' asks Waldo in the poem which was quoted at the beginning

> Beth yw adnabod? Cael un gwraidd
>   Dan y canghennau.

'To find the one root under the branches'; the one root of God's image and likeness under all the broken branches of the tree of man; the one root of the light of Christ and the life of the Holy Spirit under all the fractured branches of the tree of the Church; the one glory of the Creator of all things, shining out in all the varied beauty of his creation, reflected so truly yet so diversely in the unveiled faces of a great cloud of witnesses.

NOTES

1. Waldo Williams's poems are to be found in the one volume which he published *Dail Pren* (2nd Edn. Aberystwyth 1957) p. 67. A good account of the life and work of Waldo is to be found in James Nicholas's book, *Waldo Williams*, in the 'Writers of Wales' Series (University of Wales Press 1975).

2. cf. for instance, Sermon IV on the Nativity where Andrewes says 'And here now at this word "made of a woman", he beginneth to concern us somewhat. There groweth an alliance between us ...' (*Complete Works*, L.A.C.T. Vol. I p. 55) and Sermon XI in the same series where he exclaims 'Oh how loving a knot! how by all means to be maintained! how great a pity to part it.' (ibid, p. 194).

3. R. A. Durr, *On the Mystical Poetry of Henry Vaughan* (Cambridge, Mass. 1962) pp. 24–5.

4. *The Works of Henry Vaughan* (ed. L. C. Martin) 2nd Edn. (Oxford 1957) p. 470. Further references to Henry Vaughan's writings will be to this edition.

5. Unpublished letter of 25.4.64. I am grateful to the Trustees of the Merton Legacy for permission to quote from these unpublished letters.

6. Thomas Merton, *Conjectures of a Guilty Bystander* (New York, 1966) p. 12.

7. Letter of 21.10.63.

8. op. cit pp. 181–2.

9. Letter of 10.7.67.

10. Thomas Merton, *The Geography of Lograire*, pp. 3–5. Can one see an influence of the opening sections of David Jones's *The Anathemata*, in this prologue? Must one not, despite Merton's reported disclaimer, see some reminiscence of the Welsh name for England, *Lloegr* (in medieval French and English *Logres*) in the title of the poem?

11. Jeremy Hooker, *David Jones, An Exploratory Study* (London 1975) p. 9.

11a. For an account of Eucherius and his period see N. K. Chadwick, *Poetry and Letters in Early Christian Gaul* (Cambridge 1955) particularly Chapter VI.

11b. For Merton's appreciation of Eucherius, see *Conjectures of a Guilty Bystander* pp. 225–6.

12. *Works* p. 352.

13. ibid, p. 326.

14. ibid, p. 540.

15. ibid, pp. 323–4.

16. ibid. pp. 329–40.

17. This particular reference to George Herbert comes in 'The Mount of Olives' (*Works*, p. 186) and is not so far removed from Vaughan's one quotation in the 'old British tongue'. I am indebted at this point to my friend the Revd. James Coutts.

18. D. Gwenallt Jones, *Eples* (Llandysul 1951) p. 63.

19. op. cit. p. 483.

20. ibid, pp. 422–3.
21. The original with an English translation is to be found in R. Gerallt Jones (ed) *Poetry of Wales* 1930–1970 (Llandysul, 1974) pp. 204–5.
22. E. C. Pettet, *Of Paradise and Light* (Cambridge, 1960) p. 157.
23. *Dail Pren* p. 90. R. Gerallt Jones pp. 214–15.
24. op. cit. p. 352.

10

A Discovery of David Jones

Very gradually the importance of the work of David Jones, both as writer and artist, is coming to be more widely recognised. His major works *The Anathemata* and *In Parenthesis*, and the collection of his essays and papers entitled *Epoch and Artist*, are all available in paperback.[1] In 1971, the first full-length study of his work was published, David Blamires's *David Jones, Artist and Writer* (Manchester University Press). Dr Blamires's book provides an invaluable survey, perceptive and balanced, both of the writings and of the drawings and paintings of this still neglected maker. Its publication marked a significant step in the growth of public understanding and appreciation. So far as the visual element of David Jones's work is concerned, the various exhibitions which have been organised in recent years have revealed something of its richness and variety. Who is this man, whose name is still unfamiliar to so many, but who has so strong a hold on his admirers, and why should his work be of particular interest to those who are in any way concerned with theology?

David Jones was a London Welshman; that is to say that he was born and lived most of his life in London, but he remained very conscious that Wales, his father's country, was in a sense his own home country. He fought as a private soldier in the first World War and was wounded in it. In the 1920s he became a Roman Catholic and was closely associated with a group of artists of whom the most famous was Eric Gill. It was not until 1936 that his first book appeared. *In Parenthesis* was recognised at once by T. S. Eliot as one of the major poetic works of our century. After the second World War his larger and more complex work *The Anathemata* was published. In 1967 a special number of the poetry magazine *Agenda* appeared, containing a collection of discerning studies of various aspects of David Jones's activity as a maker. In the year of his death, 1974, a further volume of poetic work was published, *The Sleeping Lord, and Other Fragments*. These, taken with the study by Dr Blamires, and the essays in *Epoch and Artist* can provide a way into the reading of this admittedly difficult writer.

It must be said at the outset that the work of David Jones, both in writing and in the visual arts, is concerned throughout with the vision of this world as God's world. Two of the central themes in his activity are sacrament and anamnesis. Heaven and earth are full of God's glory. But it is really this earth in which the glory is to be revealed, not some fantasy world, nor some select and insulated corner of the whole of reality. *In Parenthesis* is a book about the experience of a young infantryman in the trenches of Flanders in 1915 and 1916. There is no attempt to romanticise the reality, still less to be sentimental about it. There is however a very intense attempt to see in it some signs of the redeeming, integrating mercy of God, to see the goodness, the truth and even the beauty which are present in the most apparently unpromising areas of human life. To have looked with such honesty and such compassion, to have seen so much and not to have become hardened, these are things for which one can only feel grateful to the writer; they enlarge one's own capacity for seeing. Already in a reading of this first work one becomes aware of coming into contact with a writer who can alter one's whole way of seeing things.

The Anathemata is a larger, more ambitious, more difficult work. *In Parenthesis* is a work of personal anamnesis, the result of a remembering of many things which it would have been easier to forget. *The Anathemata* is a work of a more universal recollection. It is concerned with the memory of Britain, and with the many different peoples who have had a part in its development and making. But it looks back behind historic time to pre-historic, and behind the pre-historic to the geological eras. Like Teilhard de Chardin, David Jones enables us to incorporate into our vision of the world something of its size and age which modern science has disclosed to us. These are still largely unassimilated discoveries. 'Even as an archaeologist', writes Stuart Piggott, Professor of Archaeology in Edinburgh University, 'I should hardly have thought the Quaternary Period a subject for more than the most disastrous and pedestrian verse ... David Jones has transmuted the Pleistocene into pure poetry.' [2]

But this enlargement of vision does not blur the edges, or end up in vague generalities. The artist must always see things clearly; sacraments are always particular, concrete, embodied things. This is particularly true in the work of David Jones. Stuart Piggott again makes an observation which could be of very great value for anyone trying to study the Bible or Church history. 'To be intensely poetic about the past without any lapse into sentimentality is no easy thing. It can only come from an intellectual honesty leading to a determination to try to see each aspect of the past in its own terms, and not in the false terms of one's own presuppositions, which reduce the past into something safe and ordinary, instead of extraordinary, diverse and challenging.' [3] It is only too easy to project our own conceptions, our own preoccupations, onto the past, so as to make it more manageable and comfortable, and thus to fail to see it in all its peculiar strangeness and glory.

This love for the uniqueness, the specificity, of things is one of the qualities David Jones shares with another poet, Gerard Manley Hopkins, who was also much concerned with the sacramental nature of the world, and who was also deeply influenced by the tradition of Wales. Hopkins glorifies God in 'all trades, their gear and tackle and trim. All things counter, original, spare, strange', and David Jones does the same, both in his writing and in his painting. Lord Clark, describing one of his outstanding paintings, says: 'As in all David Jones's work the sharpness of focus with which the details are seen varies from inch to inch. I am reminded of the hours I used to spend fishing off the coast of Skye, when, on calm days, one could look down many fathoms to gently undulating streamers of weed, sea-urchins, sea-anemones and puffs of sand, where the furtive flounder burrowed its way out of sight. Then a breeze would ruffle the surface and this garden of delights would be disturbed, but through a window of calm water one could still catch sight of certain man-defined objects, an old anchor or a discarded rowlock. So, in David Jones's drawing, the welter of clouds, sea gulls, and stars that surrounds Tristan's ship seems to be ruffled by the wind, but on the ship itself the mechanism of sail is clear, with anchors, blocks, and a contrivance known as a knight-head, drawn as sharply as Iseult's foot.' [4] This picture, which shows the two lovers Tristan and Iseult drinking the love potion, is so full of detail that at first approach it seems simply baffling. The secret is to take time, to let it make its own impression; gradually to allow the details to relate to one another, until suddenly any number of things in it became clear, the ship, the lovers, the various attendant figures, all the circumstances of that one unique moment.

One can have a similar impression with his writings. At first there may be only a few things which come sharply into focus. Much is unclear; there is so much detail; it is difficult to place oneself in such a rich and complex universe. The texture of the writing has as many dimensions as the reality it describes. Again, the secret is to take time. No one could hope to read these poems and understand them all at once. We have to learn not only to see what they say, but how they say it. But the first tantalising glimpses of clarity may be enough to lure the reader on, on into the footnotes or into the geological and anthropological references, on into the unravelling of phrases of liturgical Latin or medieval Welsh, so that gradually, through attention to the detail, one learns eventually to attend from the detail back to the picture as a whole, but now seen in more of its richness and diversity, and its strangely irregular underlying order. For David Jones is one who is determined to gather up the fragments so that nothing be lost, as he himself writes in one place: 'Gathering all things in, twining each trussed stem to the swaying trellis of the dance, the dance about the sawn lode-stake on the hill where the hidden stillness is at the core of the struggle. . . .'

One of the most important contributions of David Jones's work to the recovery of theological understanding lies in the suggestions which it contains of how all things may be gathered in. In the present century theological thought seems to have swayed between the position of those who have stressed the specificity of the Christian revelation to such an extent as to deny any real continuity between it and the rest of human experience, and the opposed position of those who in search for a genuine universalism have been in danger of losing sight of the historical particularity and givenness of the Christian thing. In David Jones there can never be any doubt of the intention to include, rather than exclude. This is a point which Dr Blamires makes with emphasis in his study of his work. Writing of *The Anathemata* he says, 'it becomes clear that David Jones is interested in the phenomenon of religious awareness of such. As a Catholic he naturally gives pride of place to the signs and symbols and to the mythology of Christianity, but he seems hardly less interested in the myths of Greece and Rome and the rituals of pre-historic man. The conviction with which the poem carries its readers thus depends on the extent to which the poet makes living and real the multitudinous links and identifications which he himself experiences between the beliefs and practices of very various religions' (op. cit., p. 129). This is indeed well said, and the gathering together of the 'waters' which leads up to the cry *Sitio* in the last section of the poem is a remarkable instance of that gathering in.

But at the same time, and Dr Blamires does not neglect to notice this, there is in the same section an equal emphasis on the particularity and uniqueness of the one place, the one time. It is

> not on any hill
>   but on Ariel Hill

and it is

> his ninth hour out-cry . . .
> At the taking over of third day-relief
>   three hours since
> the median hour.

The inclusiveness of David Jones's vision does not blur the uniqueness of the one act of God in Christ. What it does, in ways which are frequently startling to us, is to show us something of the extent to which that uniqueness is inclusive not exclusive, revealing how all things relate to the one central point of redemption and healing. It is in this sense that 'The whole of life and experience is, for David Jones, sacramental . . . , and everything is seen in the setting that is crowned in Christianity by the rite variously referred to as the mass, holy communion, the Lord's supper or the breaking of bread.'⁵ One of the reflections which a reading of David Jones most frequently prompts is that we fail to appreciate the nature of the specific sacraments of the Church, whether the two or the seven, because we fail to appreciate the way in which all things are sacramental, in particular all man's acts of making. Here again, while we must not lose the specificity of baptism and eucharist, we shall hardly see their meaning until we see them in a much larger and more varied context.

But if Mr Jones's work is inescapably involved with the nature of sign and sacrament, it is no less clearly concerned with another matter, that is to say the quality of 'nowness', what he calls 'a kind of transubstantiated actual-ness'. It is concerned at one and the same time with the recalling of the past, often of the remote past, and with the quality of the present moment, its particular character and demands. This is a recurring theme in the essays in *Epoch and Artist*. On the one side we find in them fascinating discussions of the 'matter of Britain', that amalgam of history and myth which lies behind the later history of our islands. Here the intuitive perceptions of the poet are linked with the questioning mind of one who has read very extensively in the scholarly investigations of this area. We become aware of the Roman and Celtic strata underlying the surface of our over-familiar country. We learn that England is emphatically not the same as Britain, that the place where we live is older, richer, stranger than we ever knew. It is like discovering that there are rooms in the house whose existence we never suspected. But none of this writing is merely antiquarian, still less escapist. It is at the service of a rediscovery of things as they are now; it enlarges our understanding and our sympathies. In this sense it could serve as a model to the biblical scholar or the Church historian, who is also necessarily much concerned with the past, but concerned with it as it is realised in the present.

A man with such an acute awareness of the sacramental nature of things can hardly help being burdened with an almost overwhelming sense of the lack of understanding of signs and symbols which characterises our present historical moment. It is not that we fail to create symbols, but that we are so largely unconscious of what we are creating, and what our creations are saying. But where a man's

heart is, there will his treasure be also. Our priorities can be seen in
the care we give to the things we make. 'Thus we have the for-
midable beauty of the war-planes and of the ballistic devices of
various kinds. Thus, also the gleaming and exact apparatuses, the
beauty of which, being seen, pleases, even when seen from the den-
tist's chair . . .', as contrasted with 'the vacuity and deprivation apparent in the thousand-and-one utensils and impedimenta of our
daily lives, domestic or public. There the mediocre, shoddy and slick
is no longer a matter for comment.' [6] It is the kind of insight which
can be found in Thomas Merton, 'Compare our monastery and the
General Electric plant in Louisville. Which one is the more serious
and more "religious" institution? One might be tempted to say "the
monastery", out of sheer habit. But, in fact, the religious seriousness
of the monastery is like sand-lot baseball compared with the big-
league seriousness of General Electric.' [7]

In such an age, the work of the writer is confronted with special
difficulties. On the one side, he must resist the temptations to lose
sight of the past, to lose touch with the living and inward continuities which give meaning and direction to the present. On the
other, if he is to produce a work which will live, he must manage to
be wholly present in that particular moment which is given him.
'Our images, not only our ideas, must be valid *now*.' It is in this
given time that incarnation can take place, 'concept and universality
be married to the local and particular'.[8] These problems, if they
afflict the artist and the imaginative writer in one way, are certainly
not unfamiliar to the theologian. He too knows the perils of a loss of
memory. He knows the no less serious dangers of a flight into
archaism or romanticism. To make anamnesis involves a recalling of
the reality of the past so that it becomes truly present and life-giving
now, so opening the way towards the unexpectedness of the future.
In trying to see how we may let the Spirit make this anamnesis in us,
we shall find much that is illuminating in the making of this writer.

There are many other aspects of the work of David Jones which
would be of value to the Christian who is trying to reflect on the
meaning of his faith. One which at least must be mentioned arises
out of his vision of the holiness, the worth of all the most common
objects. We shall have to make an enormous adjustment in our
habits of thought and action if we are to avert the environmental

catastrophe which threatens us. One thing which will be necessary will be a new sense of the value of material things. A theology of things and of man as creator and maker with God is clearly demanded of us; at least some hints towards it are to be found here.

But it would be more valuable to give at least one extended quotation from the work of David Jones so as to give some idea of the quality of his writing. Amongst the fragments which are published in the volume called *The Sleeping Lord* is one piece which is particularly direct and powerful. It is called 'The Hunt', and it refers to the story of the hunting of the *Twrch Trwyth*, one of the Arthurian passages to be found in the *Mabinogion*. The King, with his nobles, and with allies from neighbouring lands, sets out to hunt an enormous hog, the Twrch Trwyth, which has been ravaging the south of Britain. Arthur here is the type of man in his kingly dignity, man as ruler confronting the forces of chaos and destruction which constantly menace human life and society; he is evidently the type of Christ, the suffering redeemer; but he is also the 'man in the green', the green man of medieval mythology, who is the personification of the forces of growth and renewal in creation, for creation and redemption alike proceed from a single hand. But it is much better to let the poetry speak for itself. He is speaking of Arthur,

the diademed leader
   who directs the toil
   whose face is furrowed
with the weight of the enterprise
the lord of the conspicious scars whose visage is fouled
with the hog-spittle, whose cheeks are fretted with
the grime of the hunt-toil:
   if his forehead is radiant
like the smooth hill in the lateral light
   it is corrugated
like the defences of the hill
   because of his care for the land
and for the men of land.
   If his eyes are narrowed for the stress of the hunt
and because of the hog, they are moist for the ruin

and for love of the recumbant bodies that strew
the ruin.

If his embroidered habit is clearly from a palace
wardrobe it is mired and rent, and his bruised limbs
gleam from between the rents, by reason of the excessive
fury of his riding when he rode the close thicket as
though it were an open launde

(indeed, was it he riding the forest-ride, or was
the tangled forest riding?)

for the thorns and the flowers of the forest and
the bright elm-shoots and the twisted tanglewood of
stamen and stem clung and meshed him and starred him
with variety

and the green tendrils gartered him and briary —
loops galloon him with splinter-spike and broken blossom
twining his royal needlework,

and ruby petal-points counter
the countless points of his wounds,

and from his lifted cranium where the priced tresses
dragged with sweat stray his straight brow-furrows
under the twisted diadem

to the numbered bones
of his scarred feet,

and from the saturated forelock
of his maned mare

to her streaming flanks
and in broken festoons for her quivering fetlocks
he was caparison'd in the flora

of the woodlands of Britain,
and like a stricken numen of the woods

he rode
with the trophies of the woods

upon him
who rode

for the healing of the woods
and because of the hog.

Like the breast of the cock-thrush that is torn
in the hedge-war when bright on the native mottle

the deeper mottling is, and brighting the diversity of
textures and crystal bright on the delicate fret the
clear dew-drops gleam; so was his dappling and his
dreadful variety
the speckled lord of Prydain
in his twice-embroidered coat
  the bleeding man in the green,
  and if through the trellis of green
  and between the rents of the needlework
the whiteness of his body shone
  so did his dark wounds glisten.
And if his eyes, from their scrutiny of the hog-track
and from considering the hog, turned to consider the
men of the host (so that the eyes of the men of the
host met his eyes) it would be difficult to speak of
so extreme a metamorphosis.
  When they paused at the check
when they drew breath
And the sweat of the men and the horses salted the
dew of the forest floor and the hard breathing of the many
men and of the many dogs and of the horses woke the
fauna cry of the Great Forest and shook the silent
flora.
  And the extremity of anger
alternating with sorrow
  on the furrowed faces
of the Arya
  transmogrified the calm face
of the morning
as when a change-wind stirs
and the colours change in the boding thundercalm
  because this was the day
of the Passion of the Men of Britain
  when they hunted the Hog
life for life. [9]

In this passage one sees yet again how the figure of Arthur is
capable of coming to life in our own time. One sees also a little of

David Jones's intense concern to show that the island of Britain is more than England, a fact which means that the English must learn a new understanding and a new appreciation of Wales and of the things of Wales if they are not to destroy something which lies at the roots of their own heritage. Above all, one sees, as in all his writing, a vision of how suffering may be redemptive, and how even in most desperate straits man and the creation are never wholly abandoned by the creative and renewing power of God.

NOTES

1. All published by Faber and Faber.
2. *Agenda*, Spring–Summer 1967 p. 77.
3. ibid. p. 79.
4. ibid. p. 98.
5. ibid. p. 29.
6. op. cit. p. 181.
7. Thomas Merton, *Conjectures of a Guilty Bystander* p. 211.
8. *Epoch and Artist* p. 210.
9. *The Sleeping Lord* pp. 65–7.

Index

DATE DUE

DEMCO 38-297